May you always love
as if you've never
been hurt

Barbara Boatright

Impaled on the Horns Of the Devil

The Development of Vulnerability to an Abusive Marriage

BARBARA BOATRIGHT

Cover and Interior Art
Jenni Conway, eatlotsamangos@gmail

authorHOUSE®

AuthorHouse™
1663 Liberty Drive
Bloomington, IN 47403
www.authorhouse.com
Phone: 1-800-839-8640

First published by AuthorHouse 7/11/2011

ISBN: 978-1-4567-5368-9 (e)
ISBN: 978-1-4567-5366-5 (hc)
ISBN: 978-1-4567-5367-2 (sc)

Library of Congress Control Number: 2011907669

Printed in the United States of America

Dedication

To my husband, Carl Boatright

He has loved me and held to my best interest for more than fifty years. He has encouraged me in my scholastic endeavors and respected my need for intellectual independence. He has put up with most of my creative endeavors, but most of all, he has wholeheartedly supported me in my teaching and in the writing of this book.

He is my anchor and my lover.

Acknowledgments

ORGANIZATIONS:

Gary Public School System   1935-1947

English Teachers
Osher Program, UCSan Marcos   Professor, Brandon Cesmat
Emmanuel Faith Community   ChurchPastoral staff
Emmanuel Faith Women's Monday Morning   Bible Study Group
North County Writers' Bloc   Critique group
Carol Saylor (retired professor)   Critique group leader

PUBLISHERS AND WRITERS OF SAN DIEGO
ENCOURAGERS: All of the Above, plus:

Mother   Dorothy Conway
Husband   Carl Boatright
Sister   Bert Anderson
Brothers John and Milt Conway
Sister-in-law   Janet Conway
         Dr. Wilhelmina Nielson
         Dr. Helen McEuen,

FRIENDS AND HELPERS:

Sharon Brown
Vivian Holland
Judy Chavez, tech guru
Nieces Kathy Mehlhop and Jenni Conway

Disclaimer:

The events in this book are absolutely true, to the best of my recollection. However, to engage and hold the reader's attention, some of the material is presented as stories rather than simply narration or exposition. This necessitates the construction of conversations from long ago that cannot possibly be quotations. The dialogue is plausible, reflecting what I remember as the speaker's intent. It is designed only as a vehicle to illustrate characterizations, relationships, and situations between myself and actual people in my past.

Today this form of "Memoir" is known as "Creative Non-fiction!"

With this as an introduction, I humbly offer my readers the following memoir entitled:

IMPALED ON THE HORNS OF THE DEVIL

Barbara Boatright
February, 2011.

Table of Contents

PART ONE

Impaled...

Be of sober spirit,
be on the alert.
Your adversary,
the devil,
prowls about,
like a roaring lion
seeking someone to devour.

1 Peter 5:8 New American Standard Bible

Chapter One

The Seduction

Wintertime, 1951, Gary, Indiana

His left arm brushed so lightly against mine that I knew it was an accident. We were sitting in a hot and stuffy classroom and it was filled with desks. Each desk had a small writing table attached to its right arm, and every one of the desks was filled with a student. Since we were very crowded, some physical contact was inevitable. I tried to ignore his elbow on my armrest, and to concentrate on what the teacher was saying. The teacher was very interesting, I told myself...

I returned for the next class meeting and, as usual, I sat in a desk on the right side of the first row so that the teacher was speaking on my left and so that I would be able to hear as well as possible. That same guy sat next to me again, on my right. He made me nervous being there because my hearing was very poor, especially in the right ear. If he tried to talk to me I would have a hard time understanding him, and I'd be embarrassed, as usual.

Oh, well, we'll be so busy listening to the teacher that we won't have time to visit. Besides, what I had seen of him so far, I couldn't care less.

Some minutes later, after the teacher began talking, my neighbor shifted position in his desk, and he "invaded" my space again. I continued to look straight ahead, totally ignoring him and he seemed to ignore me. Finally, my curiosity got the best of me and I began to steal furtive glances at him, all of the time appearing to give my full attention to the teacher. He wasn't much to look at, really. He was kinda short, not at all muscular. His thin light brown hair hung limply but it was cut in a conservative manner. He wore dark dress pants and a muted colored sport shirt, when everyone else was wearing jeans and just plain tee shirts. He looked like he was a non-conformist and that he deliberately dressed differently than the rest of the fellows in the class. He concentrated so hard on the teacher, that I assumed he was a sincere student like I. I really wasn't interested in him, just curious, that's all.

In class several days later he touched my arm with his in a much more deliberate way. I became aware of a strange twinge every time he "accidentally" touched me. In my naiveté, I wondered what was going on, but I didn't do anything to stop it. This was something new to me, and in a strange way it was exciting. He always looked away, focusing on the teacher. He pretended to be totally unaware of me. Then he accidentally rubbed his elbow along the full length of my forearm that was resting on my armrest between us. I finally realized, because of my physical reaction and my involuntary blushing, that he was engaging in a muted form of very suggestive flirting, and that I was letting him do it! It seemed more exciting because we were so secretive; no one else knew it was going on, not even the teacher just a few feet away.

I was feeling like a silly little teenager. The truth of the matter was that this all was taking place in college, in a night school class, and that we had signed up to learn about abnormal psychology. I was on my way to learning first hand a whole lot more about abnormal psychology than I wanted, and I wasn't going to be learning a lot of it from the professor!

We began to visit out in the hall during breaks and Floyd intrigued me because he was so very different from my husband. He seemed to be a sincere student who said he valued higher education and was supportive of women having careers especially in teaching, because it was so altruistic. He claimed that he wanted to get a degree in Sociology and Psychology and to become a social worker and counselor. As we got better acquainted, it seemed to me that he was everything that Johnny wasn't, and this realization simply fed the discontent that I was experiencing at home.

Chapter Two

Coffee Klatch

I leaned against the wall and Floyd stood in front of me. His feet were far apart and I felt all boxed in. I was uncomfortable. It seemed like he was towering over me even if he was only a few inches taller than my five feet four. We were visiting in the hall during the class break one evening.

He's looking me over. I wish I didn't look so much like a kid. This blue corduroy skirt and sweater are clothes left over from my college days. Except for the white bobby socks and loafers I'm wearing tonight, it was what I wore to teach in today. Of course, the socks and loafers don't show anyway because I had to wear boots over them. I wish I had some more professional looking clothes. Oh, well, tonight I'm a student again, after all.

Running his finger over his eyebrows called my attention to his steely blue eyes. "How about letting me buy you a cup of coffee after class while you wait for your bus?"

Gee, looks like he wants to spend more time with me. That's great! I'm really curious about him. He's so different- The coffee shop will be warm. A lot better than freezing to death on the street corner in this blizzard.

"That sounds great. My husband won't be worrying about me being out in this storm because he's not home yet. He's working 4 to 12 this week." (That's Gary, Indiana talk for the three shifts that keep the steel mills up and running 24 hours a day.) "We don't get to see much of each other on this shift because of my teaching during the day, but we make up for it on the week ends!"

There, that should let him know that I am happily married and that I am school teacher. He can't say I'm flying under false colors. No sense in even visiting with him if that scares him off.

Outside, a lashing wind was blowing hard grainy snowflakes in from Lake Michigan. Floyd and I gasped as we strained against the biting wind.

Why didn't I wear snow pants or leggings tonight? The wind is wrapping my skirt around my bare legs. I think I'm going to freeze to death!

We hurried to the coffee shop. We stumbled in, stomping the snow off of our boots in the entryway. We hung our heavy coats, caps and mufflers on hooks near the front door and stuffed our gloves into our coat pockets. The fragrance of fresh coffee brewing filled the air. This was a comfortable place to escape the bad weather. Floyd chose a large booth at the front of the café and I followed. I sat close to the plate glass window so I could look up the street to see the bus coming. There were other people waiting for it too, so when it appeared, I'd have time to scurry out and catch it.

Floyd sat down across from me and as soon as we got settled he leaned across the table toward me. "You know, this light really makes your red hair shine."

I dropped my eyes from his in shyness. "I'll take that as a complement?"

"Of course. Actually, it's not really red. You're more of a strawberry blonde. Like an Irish lassie. I guess I'll call you "Bonnie".

"Bonnie?"

"Yes, you're too young and pretty to be a Barbara."

Wow! That's the first time anyone told me I was pretty! (I learned much later that bestowing names and nicknames on another person signified ownership and dominance. Just like Adam, in naming the animals, established his dominion over them.)

"You know, with your fair skin you remind me of some of the Swedish girls I saw when I was over there last year."

Now wide-eyed and alert, I said, "You've been to Sweden? I'd love to go there. I've always wanted to do a lot of traveling."

The waitress arrived to take our orders. We both ordered black coffee. After that, Floyd got more serious and seemed to be practicing his psychological counseling on me. Somehow the way his eyes locked on mine made me feel spooky. It was as if he was reading my mind and I dare not try to keep anything from him. But I was fascinated with his intensity. It was great to have someone so interested in what I had to say.

"Bonnie, tell me about your childhood."

"My parents loved me very much. I was always such a good girl, very obedient. They always told me how proud they were of me."

"How was that?"

"I remember when I was only about four years old, before Bert, my sister, was born, Mom told me about how pleased they were in the cafeterias when we were traveling. I never acted up like some other kids did. (I never had anyone to act up with!) Mom said they could leave me sitting at the table by myself just like a young lady, while they went through the line getting our dinners. Everyone was so impressed at how grown up I acted."

Actually, I was shy and I'd do anything they asked rather than attract negative attention!

The waitress came back with our coffee. "Here you are," she said. "The cream and sugar are there on the table. Could I get you a couple of cinnamon rolls? They're fresh out of the oven."

I was seriously tempted but without consulting me, Floyd replied to her in a curt manner, "No! That's all."

He read my mind and knew I was tempted!

Then he turned to me and said, "You don't need the extra calories, you know."

I nodded my head in meek agreement, but I was really embarrassed…

Yes, I am too fat but you really didn't have say that, you know!

Continuing with our conversation, Floyd said, "What did your parents do if you didn't behave?"

"If I was really bad at home, I got a spanking, but usually out in public, just being concerned about what other people might think of me was enough to keep me in line."

"Your public image was really that important?"

"I guess so… Another time Mom wanted to cut my hair and I didn't want her to do it. I wanted braids like all of the other girls had. She set up our kitchen stool in the back yard. I'll never forget. It was on a Monday morning when all of the neighbors were out hanging up their washings. She got me to sit on the stool out there in full view of everyone. Then she started cutting my hair. She kept telling me that I didn't want the neighbors to see me being a bad girl, so I just sat there, whimpering quietly. When she was finally finished giving me a Buster Brown cut, which I hated, I ran into the house, threw myself on my bed and bawled. She came in, rubbed my back to calm me down and told me she was so proud of me because I didn't put up a fuss in front of all of our friends. But I wanted long pretty hair, not short hair, almost like a boy's, even if it was easier to take care of."

Floyd's and my first visit over coffee came to an abrupt end when my bus appeared.

"Oh, gee, here comes my bus. I hate to rush, but I gotta go! See you on Wednesday!"

I grabbed my hat, coat, muffler, and gloves. I threw them on as I rushed out, just in time to be the last one to get on the bus. The driver didn't see me coming and I was frantic because I knew I was already too late getting home from class. As I stepped up into the bus, the door began to close. I jerked my body in to clear the door and the driver almost caught my coat in the door. He laughed as though he thought it was funny. I grinned at him and said, "Made it!"

I staggered down the aisle of the lurching bus. I hunkered down in my seat and looked at the wind driven snow raging outside my window. I was already excited about our next visit. I really was flattered by his attention and his obvious desire to get acquainted with me.

Chapter Three

The Storm, Inside and Out

Floyd and I again went out for coffee after class. We sat in the same window booth as before. The storm outside was still dumping snow on northern Indiana, but this time a storm was going to start raging inside of me, too. Floyd was going to trigger it.

He sat down across from me. As soon as we got settled he said, "How long did you know Johnny before you got married?"

Before I could reply, the waitress appeared.

"Do you two want coffee? Or maybe steaming cups of hot chocolate?"

We both ordered black coffee but Floyd frowned at her intrusion because she dared to interrupt us.

He seems so impatient and rude to her, but not to me. He's so intense. I feel like he can look right through me. He demands me to be very open and honest. It's so unusual.

"As I was saying, how long did you know your husband before you married him?'

He demanded my constant attention to him. His beady little eyes seemed to bore through my skull, but then, I was flattered by how closely he listened to me. As soon as the waitress left, I said,

"A little more than five years. Johnny and I started going steady early in our junior year in high school. We had great times together and we were really in love.

"You went steady in high school?"

"My mom and dad didn't approve but it saved me from worrying about whether I would have a date for the next dance at school. I guess "going steady" is teen-age social security!"

I laughed at my little play on words but Floyd didn't react at all to my attempt to be clever. In fact, as I looked back on our conversations, I thought I never saw him laugh at anything. He seemed to be so serious, always trying to teach me something or to psychoanalyze me.

He patted my hand in a condescending manner. "Yes, I guess that would really be necessary for you because you're so unsure of yourself. I assume Johnny was also a misfit in school?"

I jerked my hand back! I was quick to deny that one! "Oh, no! Neither of us were misfits. True, Johnny was too short to be a big star in football or basketball, but he could run circles around the bigger guys. His hustle and speed threw them off balance and earned him second string positions in both of our basketball and football teams."

"But he was only second string?"

There he goes again! An implied put-down.

"Well, yes. Of course, because of his speed, he was great in track, but track events didn't attract the attention that the other sports did."

"So sports were important to you only because of Johnny?"

Is that another one?

"No, you know Wirt is the smallest high school in town. Because of that, everyone attends all of the games. My dad taught me the rules of the games when he took my girlfriends and me to football and basketball games in junior high. I was lucky. I knew more about sports than most girls.

"Johnny stood out above everyone else because of his good sportsmanship even if he wasn't a star. I was proud to be his girlfriend."

The waitress came back with our coffee. "Can I get you anything else?"

Floyd replied to her in a curt manner, "No! That's all."

I burned my tongue in my eagerness to get started in drinking my coffee. I wanted to cover up my embarrassment at how unpleasant he was being to the waitress. Floyd stirred his in a slow methodical manner, to cool it off. He seemed to be in heavy thought and I just waited, sipping my coffee. He seemed to be planning what to ask next. Then he picked up something from what I had been saying and said,

"By the way, do you know what your IQ is? I gather that Johnny isn't as much of a student as you think you are?"

My I.Q. is none of your business. Who do you think you are, my psychoanalyst?

"Johnny never was a great student. He got B's and C's in his academic classes and all A's in the extra-curricular ones. Mom and Dad and I wanted him to go to college so that we would have that in common, but he flunked out the first year. Now he seems to resent my teaching and all of the paper grading that I have to do at home at night."

Why in the world did I say that? Why am I prattling on about things like this to him? Because I like his attention?

Seeming to ignore my confession of discord, he focused on me again as he tapped his spoon on his cup. "What else was important to you in high school besides studying?"

I perked up and replied lightly, "Johnny and I loved to dance. We went to all the school parties. We were kinda the leaders of our social gang. I had a big home just made for parties. Mom and Dad encouraged me to invite my friends in for house parties whenever I wanted. We were very active and had a lot of friends."

In order to get him to talk about himself instead of always interrogating me, I said, "What was *your* childhood like, Floyd?"

"It was hell. My mom died when I was a teenager and my dad always was a tough, stern disciplinarian. He'll always be an old school German, a real Prussian."

"Do you have any brothers or sisters?"

"Yes, they're older than I. I never see them now. We don't have anything in common."

"Oh, that's too bad. I'm sorry."

"Nah, it's nothing… In high school I never learned to dance. Didn't want to bother with all that kind of stuff. And the basketball and football games were just a waste of time."

And he called me a misfit! He looks like he's a real bookworm!

Then he changed the subject back to me. He returned to his chain of thought as though I had interrupted him. Which I did! Deliberately! But it didn't work.

"Why did your mom and dad object to you dating Johnny? He seems to be a decent kind of fellow, perhaps a bit shallow but… Did you stand up to them or did you bow obediently to their wishes?"

"Well, obviously, I fought against their criticisms, because I eventually married him! But from the time we started going steady, for five years, my parents talked to me against serious involvement with Johnny. They said they liked him, that he was a good kid, and that they knew we had a lot of fun together, but over and over they tried to impress on me that" ……

Floyd interrupted me with, "I'll bet they didn't say it outright, but they probably thought he wasn't good enough for you."

I tasted my coffee, looked at the snow pecking away at the window, and stalled as I thought about whether Floyd was right. Finally I answered,

"I suppose so. They focused on the differences in our family backgrounds as to education, ambition, and stations in life. They thought he would drag me down or prevent me from being all I wanted to be. I defended my choice of Johnny as my constant and loving companion for so long that when we finally decided to get married, I couldn't follow my misgivings to cancel at the last minute. I knew we would have problems but I believed we could work them out."

"Bonnie, do you ever feel cheated because you and Johnny have so little in common? Are you sometimes sorry you married him?"

Should I admit it? To him?

"Yes, I guess so. There are times when I just can't stand to think that someday if I'm not careful, we'll end up being just like his mom and dad. Sheer boredom. They never do anything challenging or interesting. They haven't done any traveling at all except to go "back home" to southern Illinois every few years. They aren't involved in any kind of community activities or volunteer service and they never even go to church anywhere. More and more now I'm beginning to think that my folks were right."

After a pause I again tried to change the subject. I said, "What was it like in Sweden when you were there?"

"Well, Sweden really has it all together. The government takes care of everyone. Everything is free. The people don't have to worry about doctor bills because the government runs their health system. The doctors are employees of the state so the people don't have to pay them for their services. Even higher education is free for as long as you want to go to any college or university in the country.

But tell me,' he questioned, "do you have any idea why you want to travel so much. Do you wish you could run away from anything or anyone?"

There he goes again! Always looking for the negative!

"No, I just want to see as much of the world as I can. I've always enjoyed geography and I've dreamed about traveling ever since I was just a little kid."

Then Floyd asked, "Have you ever tried to figure out why you refused to take your parents advice on dating and marriage?"

"No, I guess I was just stubborn. I never confessed to them that going steady gave me a sense of confidence that I wouldn't have had otherwise."

"You know, dating is a whole lot easier in Sweden. They don't have to try to obey any antiquated morality code."

This time I did the interrupting. I tried to cover up my discomfort by being bold. I said, "And what do you mean by that?"

I fidgeted with my napkin. I was getting antsy. I didn't like where this 'chat' was heading.

"I was there in 1949. The Swedes are very progressive. A couple is free to date and do anything they wish, sexually. It's no problem if the girl gets pregnant while they are just dating. In fact, they believe it is good if they prove they can produce children before making any commitment to marriage. If they don't go ahead and get married it's OK. No stigma attached. The government will take care of the girl and her baby as long as she's single."

Then he came back at me with, "What was sex like for you when you and Johnny were dating?"

I rebelled and thought,

Now, that's going too far! He makes me think of the Boston terrier I had when we were kids. Snubs would latch on to a toy or a rope, lock his jaws and never give it up until we quit pulling against him. Was Floyd toying with me, seeing how embarrassed he could make me?

I looked around the café at other students visiting and wondered how I could get out of this conversation. If I told him it was none of his business, he'd protest that he didn't mean to be personal. He'd say he was just accumulating information to use to further his knowledge of psychology. We weren't even dating, yet mentally, he was getting way too intimate.

Oh, saved by the bus! Boy, am I glad to see it. Great timing! I can't wait to get away from his probing.

I grabbed my purse and my books. I said a hasty goodbye; I threw on my wraps and ran to be the last one to board the bus, again! I chose a seat in the back all by myself because I didn't want to acknowledge anyone else's presence. The storm in my mind was raging now. I had too many things to sort out. The half hour bus ride home should have been a welcome quiet time for me, but instead I was really disturbed.

Oh, I wish this bus would hurry up and get me home. I had no idea it was so late! If Johnny came home early from work because of the storm, he'd be so worried about me.

In spite of my concern, I began to relax in my own fog of reverie. Every once in a while I looked out the window to check on the storm. I noticed how the fresh drifting snow covered up the grimy soot of our steel mill town. The city lights glowed through the falling snow, making everything look clean and pure. I thought that's like me. I hope my enthusiastic smile also makes me look clean and pure!

Stopping after class for a cup of coffee with Floyd before catching the bus for home isn't such a bad thing to do, is it? We're just two classmates socializing a bit, aren't we? If it isn't wrong, then why do I feel like I am sneaking around? Are there times when it's OK to lie? Like now? To protect Johnny from unfounded jealousy? Because Johnny wouldn't understand? I guess he would be jealous or suspicious...

Chapter Four

From Around The Kitchen Table

RECALL 1929 -1951

Dad built our second house on Forest Avenue when I was a senior in high school. He designed a kitchen with a booth in it in order to save floor space rather than having a free-standing table and chairs. Mom painted the walls a sunny yellow and the booth became a special spot for just sitting and talking. In the evenings after the three younger kids were in bed, Mom and Dad and I liked to gather there to finish off Mom's lemon chiffon cake with the creamy lemon sauce as a topping. They drank coffee while I sipped on milk. Dad always said that the only cup of coffee that kept him awake was the one he didn't get! We spent many late nights sitting in the kitchen booth, discussing the day's activities and my future. That usually led to them trying to give me reasons to break up with Johnny. I heard Dad say several times,

"You know your mother always said I had champagne taste on a beer budget. We wanted to work and live as though we had finished our work at Purdue, but without degrees we couldn't qualify for the professional positions that we actually wanted."

Many times Mom reminded my sister and me of how desperately she wished that she could have been more than "just a housewife".

"My dream in home economics was to work in the Betty Crocker kitchens." She said that she didn't want to go into teaching, yet that was the career they encouraged me to consider.

Johnny, his parents, and nephew, 1945
John McCrillis Lockhart (Johnny Mack)
Harold and Ruth Lockhart, and Bobby

High School Graduation Picture, 1947
How I wished I looked older and more sophisticated!

When Dad went off to Purdue University, he got absolutely no emotional or financial help from his father, so he worked in the university bookstore. Mom made an application for a school loan and had to ask her dad to sign it. He refused because he had never been in debt for anything. He and Mom's older brother even built their sturdy two story house without having to borrow any money. Times were tough for her folks when she was in school and she felt guilty for needing help to augment the wages she made working in the school cafeteria.

Dad said, "But we fell in love, dropped out of school to get married and then you came along a year later. Neither of us could really afford to continue our studies. That was the end of our college educations."

Mom added, "I guess my studies at Purdue enabled me to get

a job in Chicago during the depression, but that was only in food preparation in a YMCA cafeteria."

My parents and I were very close and I tried to make them feel better about how they had lived their lives so far.

I said, "Sure, Mom, I know that's why you've always been so active in Purdue's Home Demonstration clubs. You've used your training at Purdue to help other women become better homemakers and you've been a wonderful cook and a thrifty housewife.

"And Dad, you're a great salesman and you've worked hard for us, but I've also been so proud of you because of the way you have been working in our schools. I know you feel good about helping when you represent parents' interests as city-wide PTO president. You enjoy working with teachers and principals, and they accept you just as though you were one of them. You're so comfortable there; no one knows you don't have a degree."

But, I knew what they were up to. Sooner or later they would start working on me about Johnny. Here it came! Mom started out with,

"You know, Bobbie, in today's world it's really hard on a man if his wife has more education than he has. Johnny and his parents don't seem to even think about college for him. If you marry him some day, your college degree and position as a teacher could become a major problem in your marriage. He will feel he can't keep up with you."

Dad added, "You know, it will even affect your social life because he won't have anything in common with your college friends and he'll be uncomfortable with them."

"Yes," I said. "Maybe you're right. Johnny and I have talked about it a lot and he knows I want him to go away to school, too. We can't count on any encouragement from his mom and dad, and he says they won't be able to offer him much financial help."

COLLEGE, 1947 - 1950

The summer after we graduated from high school, Johnny and I became engaged, over Mom and Dad's objections. Johnny agreed to give college a try. I realized even then that he went to college only because it was important to me. I ignored the fact that he hadn't been a really strong student in high school, but my parents and I put so much pressure on him that he agreed to go to Iowa State University to study agriculture. He said he really wished he could be a veterinarian but he doubted he could pull down the grades for that. He was put on probation after his first semester because of low grades, but he didn't tell me about that problem when we were together at home for Christmas vacation.

Then, early in the second semester of my freshman year, I received a letter from him, telling me that he had dropped out of school and that he was going to get a job in the steel mills in Gary. He said something about having an accident on his motor scooter when riding to class in a snow storm. He assured me that he was OK and so I didn't really think it was a problem. He offered no alibi or other explanation even though he knew I would be very disappointed in him. All I knew was that he had flunked out and that I was getting good grades and really enjoyed being on campus. I knew it was the end of his effort to get a college education. So much for us having a college education in common. I agreed with Mom and Dad that this inequality really could become a problem in a marriage.

Mom and Dad continued to work on me every time I came home for a week-end. They said things like,

"You know Johnny went away to college only because you pressured him."

"And, he flunked out, didn't he?"

I admitted that he never was an "A" student and didn't really plan on going to college until I made it important. But we had such good times together. We really were a good match there.

Dad replied, But "good times" isn't a strong enough basis for a healthy marriage. Do you think Johnny will always accept the fact that you are a teacher and that he wasn't successful in college? What if he becomes uncomfortable with that?"

Mom came in with, "Will he be able to enjoy your friends from college and teaching? What will he have in common with them?"

"You enjoy reading so much. Does he?"

"Will you be able to agree on a child-raising philosophy? What if he wants to start a family right away before you've had a chance to prove yourself as a teacher?"

"His family background is so different from yours, Dear. Please think it over."

Such discussions were numerous and I vigorously defended my right to marry Johnny, just as I had done about going steady. Mom and Dad loved me very much and tried to protect me from making a decision that they were sure I would regret later, but I refused to listen to their counsel. Instead I reacted against their pressure with rebellion.

What we didn't know was that they <u>were</u> influencing me, not to prevent me from marrying Johnny, but to use as justification for a divorce when the time came.

From down at Indiana University I finally wrote him a long cruel letter, a "Dear John" letter. It was truly bad. I sent a copy of it to my folks for their approval, but Mom said it was so hurtful that she cried when she read it. I had tried to make a clean break so that he wouldn't hold out hope that we would get together again, but I guess I overdid it. It was very harsh. I sent his engagement ring back to him. We both knew he had failed to fulfill one of my expectations in a husband. It was a lot harder on him than it was on me because it was his ego that suffered, not mine.

Now I was free to do some dating on campus. In the next two years I introduced several boyfriends to Mom and Dad, but they found what seemed to be valid objections to each of them. During my last year on campus I lived in my sorority house. I didn't think I could attract a fraternity guy so I began to write to Johnny again. I used "my boyfriend back home" as an alibi to cover my insecurity and fear of rejection in the fraternity dating scene.

During my junior year in college, 1950, I went home for half of a semester to do my student teaching in Gary. Johnny and I started dating again. We found we were still as much in love as ever. Back on campus to finish the semester, I asked him if I could have his engagement ring back and he brought it down to me. That weekend we eloped to Kentucky because we wouldn't have to wait in that state for three days after applying for a license.

I "borrowed" my absent roommate's big white hat with the ostrich feather plume. I thought it looked quite bridal. We drove south to the Ohio River but in our ignorance we didn't know that there were only a few bridges to cross that wide river. We chose a town that was between bridges! It was too late to go find a bridge, cross into Kentucky, and find a justice of the peace to marry us. Instead, we spent the night in an Indiana motel. We returned to Bloomington the next day. I put my roommate's white hat back where it belonged, being careful to not damage its beautiful feather. I never told anyone about our attempt to get married or about our pretend honeymoon that night.

Chapter Five

Johnny,
On Campus

SPRING 1950

Back home in Gary, Johnny and I were enjoying a beautiful spring night. Johnny parked at the beach in Marquette Park before taking me home from our date. We cuddled and smooched in his dad's brand new sky blue Plymouth. We rolled the windows down to smell the fresh lake breezes. The gentle waves twinkled in the moonlight as they broke on the sandy shore. Johnny broke the silence with,

"The lake is so beautiful. Even in a violent winter storm, but especially here tonight."

"Yes. Aren't we lucky to have grown up on the beaches of Lake Michigan?"

It was so romantic as he held me. We snuggled down in those plush seats in Johnny's dad's car. We were feeling really close and loving, but I broke the spell when I drew away from Johnny. I turned to face him and told him I needed to talk about something else that had to be cleared up between us. With what I hoped was a soft, tender voice, I said,

"Johnny, I'm really sorry that you had to drop out of school at

Iowa State. I never understood why, because I knew you could do the work. I guess you just weren't happy there."

Johnny told me with obvious agitation, "Yeh, I was miserable. It was pure hell.

"What was wrong?"

"I tried to adjust but I never felt so out of place in my whole life. What you didn't know was that I was on probation because of low grades after the first semester."

"Oh, I'm so sorry. I didn't realize…"

"I really couldn't afford to go to college, you know. I rented the cheapest room I could find, out in town, and too far out to walk to campus or to take part in any campus activities. Mom and Dad and I didn't realize that it would make a difference."

I thought about how Johnny had no preparation for going to college. He couldn't get any advice from his folks simply because they had no experience in something like that themselves. They probably just took him and his scooter to Ames, Iowa, helped him find a room, and expected him to do whatever was necessary to make a go of it.

"I roomed out in town, too. I only had to walk about a mile and a half to campus, but that wasn't too bad. It just gave me some good exercise."

"Yes, and you had Sandy for a roommate. I didn't know anyone and I was all alone. I didn't even have a roommate. No one to talk to in the evening. I didn't have a chance to get acquainted with other students."

"I never thought about that!"

"Actually, I knew I didn't belong there. I really was a fish out of water and what was worse; I had no hope that anything was going to get better."

"Oh, Johnny, I'm really very sorry. We should have both gone to I.U. Then we could have helped each other."

And Johnny summed it all up with, "But I think your folks wanted us to grow apart in separate campuses rather than grow even closer than we were."

I couldn't argue with him on that. I agreed that he had been in an impossible situation as far as becoming part of the college scene was concerned.

"Then he just about broke me up again when he said,

"Barbara, I'm really sorry I let you down. I know you and your parents think it's important that we have college in common, but that's the way it is. It really doesn't make any difference, if we love each other, does it?"

We locked in a tight embrace and I kissed him as an answer to his question. But this time he withdrew from me and said,

"I don't know why your parents give you such a rough time about us getting married. I love you so much and I'll always take good care of you and be good to you... Your mom and dad always seem to like me and make me feel welcome."

"I guess they just have never realized how much we love each other."

Our romantic mood was broken. Johnny decided it was time to take me home. We knew Mom and Dad would be waiting up for me to come in. I knew they would be sitting around the kitchen table ready for my rundown of what we had done and where we had gone on our date. I enjoyed their attention but that night I didn't want to talk to them about Johnny. I was too involved in my own thoughts about the difficulty he had been subjected to when he tried to go off to college. And I was blaming them for putting so much pressure on us to break up.

Chapter Six

Married, At Last!

August, 1950

When I came home from Indiana University for the summer before I was to start teaching in the fall, Johnny and I tried to get Mom and Dad to accept the fact that we wanted to get married. Many times when Johnny brought me home from a date, Mom and Dad would be waiting up for us. They invited Johnny to come on in and have a midnight snack with them. Our conversations were pleasant and they were cordial but whenever one of us tried to talk about getting married, they put us off and changed the subject. Finally I told them privately that we were getting married in August and that I hoped they would be there.

Just a few weeks before school started, Johnny and I were married at home. Because of Mom's and Dad's opposition I didn't dare ask them to foot the bill for a formal church wedding. I knew better than to ask for a white wedding dress, because white was symbolic of virginity. Our parents, close relatives and a few friends assembled in the living room. Johnny and the minister stood in front of the fireplace waiting me to come down the hall. Finally, Mom came back to my bedroom to see why I was delaying everything.

She said, "What's going on back here? What's that? Are you crying?"

I was sobbing! "Oh, Mom! I don't want to go through with it but I don't know what to do! I can't hurt Johnny again. He would be so crushed. I just can't do that to him. He has always been so good to me, and I've already hurt him too many times."

"I know Dear, but it's too late for that now. Dry your eyes and put some powder on them to cover the redness. I'll walk you out into the living room. Everyone is waiting for you."

Mr. and Mrs. John M. Lockhart

And so we were married despite my belated misgivings and my parents strong objections. Dad told me later that Pastor Stubbs said to him that afternoon,

"Gil, I have to tell you. Of all of the weddings I have officiated, there has only been a few that I was there reluctantly. I'm afraid this was one of them."

Of course I had no idea as to what Dad may have said to him to trigger that response. It would have been uncharacteristic for a pastor to make a remark like that just out of the blue...

We drove around Lake Michigan on our honeymoon and had a wonderful time. When we got back into town we moved into a small two room furnished apartment near the school where I would be teaching. Our apartment was so small that at night we pulled a "Murphy bed" down out of a cabinet in the living room. It filled the room so completely that we had to crawl over our bed to get to the easy chairs on the other side of the room! But it was cheap, only forty dollars a month instead of the usual sixty to eighty dollars rent for three room apartments.

I was able to start teaching in the fall with a conditional teaching certificate. We still had a shortage of teachers that had started when our young men went off to war. Some of them were studying to become teachers under the G.I. Bill. That was a government subsidy available to all ex-military so that they could go to college. But they hadn't started graduating yet. The shortage still existed. The state issued emergency permits for anyone who was willing to start teaching with outstanding credits.

I was engrossed in my teaching. I worked hard that first year trying to keep ahead of my fourth graders, writing lesson plans for unfamiliar text books in every subject, and doing a conscientious job of grading papers. In addition I was attending classes at night school two or three nights a week in order to start working off those credits that I had to earn to get a full teaching certificate.

Johnny and I were very happy early in our marriage. Little did I know that I would precipitate a break that brought us both great pain and killed our marriage.

Chapter Seven

Finances

"No, Johnny. I don't want to start going to taverns."

"But Barbara, it isn't as though we're going to do it all the time. Let's just stop and get a couple of drinks before we head home."

"But what if someone sees me going in there? In the broad day light! I'd be so embarrassed. I don't want anyone to think I'm a drunk."

"Oh, that's so silly. It's O.K. Take my word for it!"

"But I've never even been in a tavern. I won't know how to act or what to order." I was pleading and close to crying.

"Come on, Barbara. You're 22 years old. It's time you learned how the other half lives."

"But what if I do drink too much and get drunk?"

Now Johnny was getting a bit exasperated with me. "Look, he said, "I'm your husband. I'll take care of you. I'll order something for you that you will like and we'll only have one drink apiece, and then we'll go home. I promise."

So we parked along the side of Miller Tavern and I hoped no one saw us slip in the front door. It seemed dark after coming in out of the rosy glow of the setting sun. Immediately I was repulsed by the stale musky odor of beer and liquor. By the time my eyes began to adjust to the dim light, Johnny had led me to a booth and I scootched down and tried to act like I wasn't as uncomfortable as I felt.

"How about it if I order you a rum and coke? You like cokes, don't you?"

I nodded "yes", and Johnny continued, "I'll go over to the bar and tell Joe to fix one for you and I'll get a beer for myself." He left me sitting there all by myself.

Oh, no! He even knows the bartender's name! I wonder how often he comes in here for a drink before he comes home. But, I'm just being suspicious. I never smell liquor on his breath. Now, quit worrying!

Johnny came back with our drinks. I sipped my rum and coke and agreed that it tasted fine. He was pleased.

"You, know Johnny, I feel like your mother does when she tries to talk you or your brother Wayne into buying rum for her fruit cakes every fall. She's always so afraid someone will see her going in to the liquor store right there on Lake Street."

"Yeh, we always have a good time teasing her about it. We make her bite the bullet and get it for herself! She sure makes good fruit cake though."

I looked around the smoky, stinking tavern. There weren't many customers at this time in the afternoon. We had some privacy in our booth. Maybe this would be a good time to talk finances.

"Johnny, it's great that you have a good job in the tin mill that pays so well. With your paychecks from the mill and mine from teaching we should be sitting pretty good."

"Yep, but first thing we have to do is pay off your school debt."

Johnny was frugal and wanted to pay off my school debt in the first year, but I wanted some new clothes for teaching. He said we couldn't afford them.

"But I'm embarrassed at my school girl clothing of printed cotton skirts and plain colored blouses and sweaters. I can't wear my bobby socks and loafers. I have to buy hose for teaching. But right now I need some new professional looking clothes that are more appropriate in the classroom."

"No, you look just fine to me. Maybe after I get your debt paid off.."

"Oh, Johnny, it's only $800. The terms say that I don't have to pay it back for five years after I start teaching.

"But Barbara, you know that $800 equals a little more than 40% of your yearly salary, before taxes. That's quite a chunk and the sooner we get it paid off, the better. I don't like to be in debt for anything except perhaps a mortgage some day soon. We'll always pay cash for everything."

I was compliant and saw the wisdom in Johnny's goal of paying off my school loans. Teaching was so important to me that I said I would teach if all I got as a salary was enough money to buy my hose. That's just about all I saw of my paycheck that first year.

I never thought about the role I expected Johnny would take in our life together. I assumed that he would continue to work in the steel mills just like 30% of the men in Gary, Indiana. The mills paid good wages and we would live in Gary the rest of our lives. Little did I know about the plans that Johnny had for us.

Chapter Eight

Family, Now?

Johnny and I apparently decided to let the topic of finances rest for awhile. But we weren't finished with revealing our expectations of each other. In our immaturity we hadn't discussed them before we decided to get married. Now we were still sitting in Miller Tavern.

Johnny shocked me when he said, "Next year, as soon as we get your debt paid off, then you can stay home and we'll start our family".

"Oh, no! Not so soon!" I thought. I sipped on my rum and coke while I tried to figure out how to tell him what my plans were, about having a family.

I've told everyone about how I've scheduled having a family and still being a teacher. Is it really possible I had never discussed it with Johnny?

But out loud I explained,

"Eventually I will want to stay home and raise a family and then go back to teaching when our youngest child enters school. But first I want to use my training while it is still fresh and get myself established with a good reputation in teaching."

"And how long do you think that will take?"

Johnny's voice had a hint of anger in it and he got up to get himself another beer. He didn't even look at my glass to see if I was ready for another drink. The coke had turned sour, anyway.

When he returned, I tried to reassure him with, "Probably after 5 years I'll be ready to stay home and not teach?"

"Well, we'll have to see about that. By then maybe we will have saved enough so that we can put some money down on a little farm someplace".

A farm?? Me? A farmer's wife? But I'm a school teacher! I have no intention of working like Aunt Inez and Uncle Bob had to do to feed their seven kids! There's no way I'm going to get stuck on a farm like theirs for the rest of my life!

Then I realized that I never seriously considered Johnny's desire to become a full time farmer and I couldn't picture myself in the full time role of a farmer's wife. It never occurred to me that I could live in on a farm and not have to spend all of my days surviving on my gardening, canning our produce, and slopping the hogs. But the time for a rational discussion had passed. Johnny gulped down the rest of his beer and said, "Let's get out of here."

In submission, I tagged along after him to the car. That ended our communications about our plans for the future.

Many years later, I recognized that if I had truly been living as a godly wife, I would have honored Johnny's goals and recognized that living on a farm was not necessarily living as my Aunt Inez lived. I could enjoy living as a mother and a farmer's wife first. As for my career as a teacher, after our children were all in school, I could go into town to teach school and contribute to our financial welfare in that way. I would have had the children of my own that I had always dreamed of having, rather than longing to fill that need for the rest of my adult life. I wouldn't have needed to pour all of my love for children into my students in my classroom and into Jim, (my stepson), as substitutes for "the real thing."

Growing Discord

One evening while I was doing my school work at the kitchen table, Johnny was reading a magazine. I heard hearty laughter coming from the living room and the sound of a page being ripped out of his *Saturday Evening Post.*

'Hey, look at this!" he said. "Here's a cartoon that's just a riot! It shows a hen with a red comb in her head, in a red plaid housewife's apron and she has her "hands" on her hips. She's angry and she's squawking at her rooster."

After another fit of laughter, he handed it to me. The caption below the cartoon said, "The Red-headed Henpecker". Johnny thought it was so funny. I laughed with him but didn't admit that he thought it was about me. I saved it in my cookbook just to remind me. It's still there today, as a warning and reminder, and my hair is still red!

Once when I had a bad headache I lay on the couch with my head on Johnny's lap. I didn't have any energy and was feeling weak and limp. In a tender and caring moment Johnny forgot that I was sick and said, "Gee, I wish you were like this all of the time." What he meant was that he liked it when I was docile and quiet and not trying to be in control. I wasn't griping, or finding fault. He was enjoying a peaceful and quiet wife for a change.

Another evening we were playing cards with Aunt Mary and Uncle Milt at their house. Johnny and I were pecking away at each other, this time about cards.

"Johnny, I knew you weren't going to make that contract. You should have let Uncle Milt have it, then he would have gone down, instead of us."

"I would have made it if you hadn't given me a bum steer with your bidding."

"So, it's all my fault! We never have used the same code in our bidding, have we?"

"If only you'd make some effort to remember….."

Aunt Mary interrupted us. "Come on you two! Cut it out! You're at each other's throats every time we get together. That's no way to live. If your marriage is as bad as you make it sound, maybe you should both just call it quits and get a divorce!"

If it was her intent to shock us into being civil to each other, she succeeded. I knew she didn't really mean it. She just wanted to shake us up, to show us what poor company we were. We both apologized. We were embarrassed and we tried to go on with the card game as though nothing had happened.

But inside, I was thinking about what was maybe the truth.

I'm really being a stinker. I'm picking on Johnny all the time. He can't do anything to please me. We're supposed to act like honeymooners for a while yet, but that mood disappeared months ago. We don't have anything in common and we can't talk to each other without fighting. I really don't know what is going to happen to us. It's a hopeless situation.

Chapter Nine

Springtime In the Dunes

One spring day in 1951, during a walk in the dunes, my 'sister-cousin' Dorothy Duke, and I were enjoying the views of patches of lavender-blue lupine right next to clumps of brilliant orange Indian paintbrush carpeting the valleys between the sand dunes. They were hardy wildflowers and they survived with long roots reaching down through the hot sand to a bit of moisture below. They also absorbed night time dew and draped themselves around any grassy hummocks that survived in the shifting sand.

But the beauties we were seeking grew with the more delicate spring flowers under the shade of sprawling oaks on the wooded dunes. As we came to our ridge of wooded dunes, we started looking for the light blue sand violets, our special spring treasures.

It was a warm, balmy day, just right for relaxing and we had some privacy for heart-to-heart talking. I told her about my night school class. I mentioned Floyd in a deliberate, off-handed way.

"Dot. I've met an interesting guy in my night school class."

She gave me a sideways glance. "Really? What's interesting about him? What's he like?"

"He's kinda strange, kinda like a real book worm. We've had some interesting conversations during our class breaks."

"What about?"

"Oh, psychology and stuff like that. He says he wants to be some kind of psychologist or counselor."

I can't tell her that I find him intriguing. I can't get up the nerve to tell her that he is anything more than just a curiosity. But I want to let her know that he exists, just in case…

Sensing something in my voice, Dot stretched her shoulders and acted like she was a bit uncomfortable. She started talking about Johnny instead.

"I'm glad that you and Johnny were finally able to go ahead and get married". She looked at me sheepishly. "I thought you gave him a rough time when we were down on campus together. I felt sorry for him."

To soften her implied criticism she put her arm through mine and cuddled a little closer.

Now, I was the one who felt uncomfortable.

Would she understand my feelings toward Johnny…? Do I even know what they are?

I drew a deep breath. "I've always loved him, but Mom and Dad"….

"I know, they always objected to him. They thought you two didn't have enough in common."

"I broke up with him twice because Mom and Dad told me that we weren't a good match…that we would have trouble because our aspirations were so different."

I sighed, remembering all of those midnight discussions around the kitchen table. They tried to convince me that they were advising me out of love and concern, while I was being very courteously defiant and not at all swayed by their arguments.

But, that's of that! I didn't come out here to dwell on the discord at home between Johnny and me.

Instead, I deliberately focused on the beauty of the dunes to fill my mind. Here with Dot in our beautiful dune land, which we both loved so much, I wanted to talk about more happy things. We stood in the shade near a clump of large, light blue, sand violets. They were in full bloom. We had timed our little foray just right.

Dot picked a single violet and wrinkled up her nose as she sniffed it. "Oh, that's so sweet! It's the essence of spring that we were looking for!"

"Aren't they beautiful," I gushed, as I ran my hand gently over the cluster of blossoms closest to me?" "?

"And they're thick enough here so that we can pick a couple of small bouquets to take home, just like we used to do when we were kids."

"Yeh!" It was my turn to pick a fragrantly sweet "snifter" for myself. "Remember how we were taught to always leave at least half the flowers on each plant so that there were some left to go to seed for next year?"

As we were picking violets we talked about the rumors that this ridge was soon going to be covered by a new housing development. It made us sad.

Dot again returned to the subject of Johnny. "Remember how your brother John looked up to Johnny and almost idolized him? Didn't Johnny get him the job of water boy for your football team?"

"Yes, and he was just a little 9 year old. He struggled to carry that heavy bucket of water out to the big guys whenever there was a timeout. They only had one dipper for all them use. They weren't much concerned about spreading germs in those days… because they were tough! Anyway, Johnny said every time he turned around, John was following him like a little brother would.

"And I guess Johnny felt responsible for him?"

"John told me just recently that Johnny even protected him from a bully who always gave him a hard time."

Then Dot reminded me about something that happened when I was down on campus that last spring.

"And then there's what he did for Bert in her senior year in high school. I guess he felt sorry for her because it looked like she wasn't going to get a date for her senior prom. You weren't even home because you were down on campus, but he knew about Bert not having a date.

"He wrote to me and asked me if he could take her to the prom!"

I raised my eyebrows and grinned at Dot as she continued, "Bert says it was all his idea, not something your mom or dad arranged. He said he didn't want her to miss the senior prom because it's such a big thing for girls.

"That was so sensitive of him. He always has been so kind to everyone." I gulped and tried to keep tears from springing up from deep within me. "He told me that Mom said, 'After all, you're part of the family!' So Mom made Bert a beautiful prom dress and Johnny brought her a corsage and everything. Bert said they had a great time together."

"You know, Bobbie", Dot said, "It's no wonder that he doesn't know where he stands with your folks."

"You're right! They always welcomed him as my boyfriend; I just wish they had taken our love seriously when we were teens. Lots of teens fall in love and eventually get married and live happily ever after…and, I've always loved him so much."

Chapter Ten

Wintertime
In Iowa

SPRING, 1951 (RECALL 1946 - 1948)

Settling down on a large patch of grass, I made room for her to join me. "Say, Dot, do you remember the little red scooter Johnny had?"

"Yeh, he used to pick you up in downtown Gary when you got off work at night after working all day in Gordon's," (a fine department store in downtown Gary). She giggled, and continued, "Was it really true that you thought it was funny to walk out of the store to Johnny on his scooter, along with all the sophisticated ladies that you clerked with at Gordon's?"

"Sure did!" Dot and I both laughed at the memory. "Those clerks on the first floor in cosmetics and accessories had to wear black dresses and high heels. And stand all day long behind their counters with no place to sit down! I worked on the second floor in yard goods and notions (fabric for sewing and buttons and thread, etc.) so I just wore my school clothes. Johnny was among the guys waiting for their dates, when the store closed at nine o'clock. I bounced out of there in my loafers and climbed on the back of his scooter right there in the front of the store on Broadway. I lost all pretense of sophistication. I never <u>was</u> sophisticated anyway, and didn't even want to be!"

Dot and I laughed so hard I had to gasp for breath. Then I said, "We thought it was a riot to roar away on his scooter while the other couples strolled hand in hand to their fancy sedans in the parking lot. We had a blast on that little scooter, when Mom and Dad weren't looking!" I sobered up with, "They thought it was too dangerous to ride it on Route 20, but that was the only route from downtown to the lake front."

Dot added, "and a whole lot more fun to have Johnny waiting for you rather than catching the bus!

After a pause she said, "Bobbie, Didn't he take his scooter out to Iowa when he went away to college?"

My imagination took off when I thought about riding a scooter in the dead of winter. "You know, Dot, I didn't think about it at the time, but that was the only way Johnny could get to class. I don't know if bus transportation was available, but it was in a snowstorm when he had his accident."

She whipped her head around to look at me with startled eyes. "What accident?"

"Well, he lost control of his bike on ice and slid into the car in front of him. He had a terrible deep gash on his arm and he totaled his scooter. Actually, I think that was probably the last straw for him on going to college. He lost more than a week of classes because of doctor's appointments, the stitches and the damage to his arm and he didn't have any transportation to classes. He was behind in his class work. He just gave up and came home."

Dot's eyes snapped. "Well, I don't blame him. That was tough! Can you imagine going any distance on a scooter, in the winter?"

Isn't it cute the way she is always defending him?

"I don't blame him either. I just felt so sorry for him. He didn't have a chance. And to think he went away to school only because we put so much pressure on him."

"Have you ever told him how you feel about it?"

"Yes, one night as we were parking at the beach he told me all about it. He wound it up with, "When I dropped out of school I knew you'd really be mad but I just wasn't cut out for college like you are. So I gave up. I dropped out and came home."

"And what did you say to all of that?" my cousin said as though she was accusing me of something.

"I was mortified! By then, tears were streaking my makeup. I didn't know what to say. I was so ashamed that I had not been aware of all that he had endured just because he wanted to please me. Well, Johnny loaned me his handkerchief. Finally I gained control of myself and told him that I wasn't mad, just disappointed. I said I had no idea he had such a rough time away at school. And I agreed that he had been in an impossible situation as far as becoming part of the college scene was concerned."

"I can imagine how terrible you must have felt."

Dot let out a soft "Wow!" and pretended to not notice me wiping my tear-streaked cheeks with the back of my hand. I jumped up, kinda shook myself like I had a shiver, and said, too brightly, "Well, we'd better get going. We each have a supper to get."

We trudged through the loose sand, clutching our little bunches of sand violets to show Dot's mom, my Aunt Mary. I took mine home, put them in an empty salt shaker, and decorated our kitchen table with them. Johnny came home and knew immediately what a treasure they were. We made plans to go out together to Indiana Dunes State Park on the next day we were both off. It would be great to relive our teen romance and walk along the beach again, hand in hand…Wouldn't it?

Chapter Eleven

Misery

Dear God, Here I am,… in the old dusty laundry room,… in our apartment building,… on a perfectly good Saturday,… hanging up my washing….Like a good, responsible wife. - It's raining outside….But You and I know, I'm not a good wife, in more ways than one!

To begin with, I hate housework! I don't get a kick out of trying to have everything perfect in the house, all of the time, like some women do. I'd much rather be doing anything else, anything! This dingy old room with its cold concrete walls is so depressing. The two bare light bulbs hanging from the ceiling do nothing to brighten it up. I don't even feel like my clothes are clean, having to dry inside like this. Looks like I'll have to use it even in the summertime because there are no drying lines outside. Johnny thinks it's a waste of quarters to take our washing to the laundry mat. So here I am."

I bent over to pick up a handful of wet socks and sighing, I hung them up.

Dear Lord, I don't know why I should be so miserable. I love to cook and Johnny appreciates what I fix for him. I love my teaching and my kids at school, and most of the time, Johnny doesn't object to me doing my homework at night. But it seems that we spend too much of our time griping at each other.

Lord, You know the truth is, that I'm disappointed in what Johnny seems to want out of life. Life with him isn't going to be at all like I imagined it. Now, Floyd seems to be the exact opposite. I guess I compare

46

them and Johnny always comes out on the short end. I know it's wrong to talk against my husband to someone else, especially a man, but Floyd understands me and my life goals. Sometimes I feel so smothered by the two of them, I can't breathe, and I just don't know what to do about it.

I finished that job and went into our little kitchen nearby. As I cleaned it up I continued thinking about my position before the Lord. Not good!

God, I can't even pray for help from you because I know I'm at fault and I don't want to change! I know what your Word says about the sacrament of marriage, and I don't even want to try make this one work! I simply can't honor Johnny as my husband like I know I should, because I know we should have never gotten married in the first place. I guess I'm just stuck!

As I continued with my Saturday morning housework, I thought that I wanted to be totally honest with The Lord, at least!

Lord, only you know why I insisted on marrying Johnny. To vindicate our relationship over all of those years? To prove I wasn't pregnant and 'had to get married'? Pride? I had argued about Johnny with my folks so long. I just couldn't back down and admit they were right? But why have I been so disobedient to you? I don't know! Maybe it is all of these rationalizations.

The real root of my discontent and misery was what was developing outside of my marriage. I was getting involved with a man who was a sharp contrast to my husband. Floyd was more mature, but anti-social and a loner. He had no friends and made no effort to have any kind of positive relationship with his father, sister or brother. He had no sense of humor and never did anything for fun. He seemed to be a very serious intellectual and much more sensitive than my husband was.

As we got better acquainted, he began to point out my insecurities and psychological needs. He discussed the personality faults that he found in me, but I wasn't resistant to his observations and advice. I considered him my intellectual superior and I wanted to change and please him. I thought it became his mission to instruct me in becoming his version of a tradition-defying liberal feminist, one that he could remodel and remake at will. And I didn't resist.

Was I falling into a Pygmalion trap? Or like the musical, "My Fair Lady?

What Johnny didn't know was that my attitude became more and more negative while still married to him. At times I was under Floyd's influence, and exhibited a defiant spirit of disobedience of God, of my parents and even of society itself. Then I fought back and attempted to break the relationship with Floyd that seemed to keep me in bondage and misery. I remembered my early training and God's commands in both the Old and New Testaments of the Bible concerning marriage, but it didn't really detract me from the road I was traveling. Unconsciously then, probably to assuage my guilt, I began to find fault with Johnny in everything to justify my rebellion.

Chapter Twelve

Incompatibility
Spring, 1951

As spring came upon us and my school year was winding down, Johnny and I sat at the kitchen table. After dinner, we were actually discussing our unhappy marriage. Johnny said,

"You know, my mother said that all of our troubles would disappear if you'd just stay at home and have a baby."

I was shocked! I couldn't tell him but I thought,

That's the last thing I want right now! If I did that, I would always blame you for preventing me from becoming a career teacher. I sure don't want the kind of life that your parents have had. Your mother went to normal school to become a teacher, but I don't know that she ever used that certificate. She stayed home and had babies. That's not for me!

I knew that children should never be used as the cement to hold a marriage together. I was thankful that I was not yet pregnant. I definitely was not ready to give up my teaching, to settle down and to begin washing diapers.

I even discussed my dissatisfaction with Floyd, seeking validation from him. Of course, he agreed that I deserved better. He said that he would be much more aware of my needs and desires than Johnny could ever be because he understood me and respected my ambition and desire to serve others.

Some times when I didn't have too many books or papers to carry home from school in the evening, I would walk home instead of taking the bus. Those were the private times I use to make the transition from teacher to housewife. One spring day when the weather was particularly balmy and pleasant, I decided to enjoy a walk home. I was in a contemplative mood. I tried to think about how and why I was making such a mess out my marriage.

I knew that from the time I met Floyd, I rebelled against my parent's advice and what I knew to be God's will. My major motive was self-centered with a high interest in the excitement of forbidden sex rather than being God-centered. Sure, some immature pre-teens and teenagers are notoriously selfish and self-centered on one hand and kind, altruistic, and idealistic on the other. I was both. But after graduating from college, I should have outgrown the negative behavior. I thought I was always kind and loving to my friends, my elders, and to my cousins. But in the area of marriage, my motives seemed largely self-serving. But I was miserable in my marriage because I got to the point where I wasn't looking for any admirable qualities in my husband.

I read some time later that when selfishness intrudes in a marriage, discord and disharmony reign instead of love.

Well, that certainly is what has been happening to me. I don't give Johnny the attention and companionship that he deserves as my husband. I labor as a workaholic and put my job before my marriage. I spend too many evenings grading papers and trying to stay ahead of my fourth graders with lesson plans. I have failed to focus on Johnny as my loving husband, and on what is desirable in our marriage. I harbor negatives instead, and make him miserable, also.

In spite of the really disastrous social shame of divorce in those days, as I became more and more influenced by Floyd in our clandestine meetings after class, I became more willing to look at my marriage to

Johnny as my parents had predicted; a great mistake that would soon stifle me and prevent me from being all that I could be.

In the 1950's a philosophy developed in our culture that ran counter to all Biblical commands as to the stability of marriage. The popular belief was that once a marriage went bad there was very little that could be done to bring about a permanent repair. There seemed to be many married couples who endured loveless marriages who should have split up years ago for their own happiness. Some didn't divorce for the sake of their children, until the children were grown. Others didn't divorce because their church forbids it, yet they lived in misery for the rest of their lives. These were the cases I chose to focus on. No where in my thinking was the knowledge that God and the Holy Spirit could be enlisted to bring about genuine change in personalities that would enable marriages to be repaired and for love to be restored.

I was certain that our marriage was doomed to failure if I expected to enjoy freedom and happiness in life. I decided to get out before I got pregnant. If not, I knew I would sacrifice my own happiness rather than subject my children to live with divorced parents.

Chapter Thirteen

Divorce
May, 1951

With my mind made up, it was time to contact a lawyer. I looked up the phone number of a lawyer who used to be a classmate of my mother.

"Mr. Robb, thank you for taking this call from me. I'm Barbara Lockhart, Gilbert and Dorothy Conway's daughter."

"Well, hello, Barbara. I remember when you were just a little girl and I delivered your mail. So, now you're all grown up?"

"Well, I guess so, if that's what we call it! I want to talk to you about what I need to do to get a divorce!"

"You want to talk to me about getting a divorce?"

"Yes, I don't even know if you handle them. I'm calling you because you are a friend of Mom's and I know you'll help me if you can."

"Sure, I'll be glad to try. Do your parents know about this?"

"Well, they know that my husband and I have been having a lot of trouble. I'll let them know that I have made up my mind. Then, maybe if you contact them they will give you their version of what has been going on. That might help you."

"That sounds good. It will be good to talk to your mother again, but I wish it were under happier circumstances."

Kenneth Robb thanked me for calling him. Then he said, "I'll

52

connect you back to my secretary to make an appointment with me. In the meantime, with your permission, I'll give your mother a call."

A few days later, I entered an office building in downtown Gary. I clung to the railing as I climbed the stairs , trying to wipe away my tears and gain composure before I found the lawyer's office. I was very embarrassed. I was going to have to admit that I made a grave mistake despite my parents' efforts to steer me away from it. And, getting a divorce was truly shameful, not at all respectable. Still sniffling a bit, I entered a pleasant lounge area. It had a comfortable masculine air with black leather couches and chairs. A secretary sat at a desk in the far corner.

"Good afternoon, Mrs. Lockhart? Mr. Robb is expecting you. He'll see you in a few minutes. Would you like to take a seat while you wait?"

I looked over the selection of magazines and chose "The National Geographic Magazine". I sat down and opened it but my mind wasn't on reading. Instead, I was thinking about what a scary thing this was that I was doing.

So, here I am waiting to see Mr. Kenneth Robb, lawyer! I never thought I would be doing something like this!

When Kenneth Robb and Mom were young, they were neighbors and classmates all the way through school. Mom told me that her friend was our mailman but she knew he always wanted to be a lawyer. In those days we used to get home mail deliveries twice a day! Mom said that Kenneth was working his way through law school by working for the post office. That's why he was always reading and studying even as he walked his mail route. He looked really funny.

He had been our mailman for so long that he seemed to know how many steps there were on the main sidewalk between houses. Mr. Robb could go from a mail box on a house, down a short sidewalk to the main sidewalk out front, walk a certain number of steps to the next house's short sidewalk and then to their front door. He'd pull the mail for that house from his big leather bag, check to make sure he had it correct, drop it in the mailbox, and then go back to his walking and reading. All of the time he was walking he never looked up from his book or stepped on anyone's grass! Phenomenal!

When he finally got his degree in law, our neighborhood lost our friendly mailman. I don't know how long it took him to pass the bar because we moved out to Miller, the lakefront, in 1944, while he was still delivering mail.

Mr. Robb called me into his office, offered me a chair, and then sat down behind his desk. He started out with,

"It's good to see you again, Barbara. I think the last time I saw you, you were skinning your knees in roller skating down the sidewalk on Pierce Street."

"Yes, I guess so. Pierce Street was a good place to grow up. And I remember you reading your way through law school while delivering our mail!"

We both laughed as memories came springing to life.

"Well, let's get down to business. Tell me about your marriage. Why do you need to get a divorce?"

"My husband and I are such a bad match. Mom and Dad warned me about it over and over but I wouldn't listen to them. Our backgrounds and aspirations are so different. Our views of our future are diametrically opposed."

"Can you give me an example?"

"Well, right now, he doesn't respect my education and training and my desire to teach school. He doesn't have a college education.

He thinks all of our problems would be over if I just stayed home and had babies."

"Have you been teaching?"

"Yes, I'm just finishing up my first year. I'm teaching at Glen Park School where you and Mom went when you were in grade school!"

"That's interesting. I remember good old Glen Park School well! It looks like you consider yourself a career teacher."

"I do, but I want to teach for a while before having a family."

"I take it, you don't have any children yet?"

"No, if we had any children, I wouldn't be filing for a divorce."

"That would make a difference, would it?"

"Oh, yes, sir. Divorce is a disaster for children. I'd put up with anything to protect them from that. That's why I need a divorce now, before I get pregnant."

"Has your husband ever hit you or physically hurt you in anger?"

"No, he's really a very gentle and kind person", I admitted.

"Well, how about mental or psychological abuse from him."

"We both get mad and sometimes yell at each other. But I can't really call that mental abuse."

"Has he ever threatened you or made you fear for your safety?"

"No, never."

"Well now…We have to find some grounds for divorce or the judge won't grant you one."

"Can't I get it on just incompatibility?" I twisted in my chair and hunched up closer to his desk. I was beginning to feel desperate.

This isn't nearly as cut and dry as I thought it would be.

"No, that's not enough," Mr. Robb said. How about infidelity? Has your husband ever been unfaithful, as far as you know?"

I squirmed a bit in my chair. That hurt! I was the one who was unfaithful!

"No, not really." I was glad he hadn't asked me that question about me!

But…Let's see. What about that time he went to a prostitute's house with Russell? That wouldn't be lying. It really happened!

"But there was one time when we were out driving along the lakefront. Johnny recognized his friend Russell's car parked in front a house where Johnny said a prostitute lived. I had heard about that prostitute from Johnny. He said Russell told him about how passionate and stimulating she was. I think Johnny was comparing what Russell thought about her techniques compared to mine, and I didn't measure up. Anyway, he pulled up behind Russell's old junker of a car. He said he was going to go and get Russell because he shouldn't be there. That was his alibi.

"It seemed like he was in that house forever. I was sitting in our car imagining all kinds of things, like was she serving Johnny also? Finally the two guys came out. Russell got in his car and drove away, and we followed. Typically, Johnny and I didn't talk about it. It was my nature to avoid any kind of confrontation if at all possible. I was too hurt with what I thought happened in there, and Johnny didn't offer any explanation."

I hadn't intended to tell on Johnny like that but it just came out.

Mr. Robb sat back in his chair and made a little teepee with his hands. He was thinking. Finally he said,

"From what your mother said, it sounds like Johnny won't contest a divorce."

"No, he joined the army and now he is in basic training."

"Well, if you really think he won't contest it, we'll claim irreconcilable differences and hope the judge doesn't ask too many questions. Does that sound O.K.?"

Mute with anxiety, I nodded in agreement.

"My secretary will set up a court date for us and notify you of it. I'll do the necessary paperwork, and I'll meet with you in the courthouse just before we go in to see the judge."

I thanked him and headed down the stairs with much lighter steps than I had coming up.

As predicted, Johnny chose not to fight me on a divorce. He signed the necessary paperwork, as witnessed by his commanding officer. The judge didn't ask any questions. The divorce was granted.

Now I was faced with the great shame of divorce, because I thought divorced women were really disgraced, and I didn't like to admit to any kind of failure.

I found it really wasn't so very hard to go back to Mom and Dad and say,

"You were right, I made a big mistake, and I am sorry I hadn't listened to you a long time ago".

Much relieved, they gave me room in the basement to store my used wedding gifts and household possessions. For the first time out of several more times in the next few years, I moved back into my old bedroom at home.

I sincerely believed that when I divorced Johnny it was protection for me against a life of abject hopelessness. I believed that without the divorce I would have to give up all of my aspirations in teaching and would have to try to become the kind of wife that Johnny's mother was. I saw her life as totally boring and lacking in any kind of intellectual growth or community involvement or expressions of altruism.

Once again I had dumped Johnny and was now free to date, this time, to date Floyd Dubois.

Part Two

Impaled
on the Horns...

But resist him,
firm in your faith,
knowing that the same experiences
of suffering
are being accomplished
by your brethren
who are in the world

1 Peter 5:9 NAS

Chapter Fourteen

Sneaking Around

SUMMER, 1951

In May Johnny and I split up and I moved back home into my old bedroom with Mom and Dad. I didn't have any savings for the summer. As soon as school was out in June I started working full time at Gordon's Department Store. The personnel director knew me well. I had worked there part time ever since I turned 16.

"Hi, Floyd. Thanks so much for picking me up after work. I don't think anyone saw me come back here to the parking lot."

I got into his car and gave him a big hug and a kiss or two. I craved his attention and really appreciated not having to go home on the bus. He drew me to him wanting more loving. I had to say,

"No, Floyd, not now. I'm too hot and sticky."

"That's OK. I can wait. How did thing go for you today?"

"It was horrible, I was miserable. Gordon's is so hot and stuffy when we have a heat wave. They close the store up at night, trapping all of the heat of the day to greet us the next morning. No relief. Having to wear hosiery all of the time doesn't help. It sure makes me glad that I can teach for a living rather than clerk in a store!"

"Well, it will be cooler out by the lake."

As he pulled out of the lot and headed toward the lakefront, he said, "I thought we might stop at Ted's Drive In for something to eat."

That's unusual. He very seldom spends any money when we're out together. Maybe that will change when we can date openly.

"Fine. That'll give us more time together. And besides I'm starving".

Soon we were at Ted's. We listened to the car hops take orders and watched them deliver food to people in their cars. We waited for our hamburgers and iced tea. I was hot and tired. The air was heavy with the odor of frying hamburgers and French fries. It made me even hungrier.

Floyd said, "How are you going to explain not showing up for dinner tonight?"

"I'll just tell Mom that when I got off work I went out with a friend and imply it was someone who I work with at Gordon's. I know it isn't fair to her but…"

"You need to be independent and not let them treat you like a child."

"I know. But it's hard. I can't admit to even knowing you until after my divorce is final. Then I can introduce you to my folks. It will be a great relief to not have to sneak around like this. I'm so afraid I'll get caught."

"Yes, but I'm not sure I even want to try to get to know them, after the way they try to control you. I'm getting sick and tired of you being so afraid of what people will think. You need to get rid of those old-fashioned ideas about how people should live."

I brushed aside my hair from my face. I didn't want to argue about it or defend myself to him. "Here comes our food. I'm glad it finally came."

"Sir, if you'll roll your window down a bit more, I'll be able to hang the tray on your car door. Thanks. Is there anything else I can get you?"

Floyd scanned the tray and said, "No, that will be all." He handed her a five dollar bill and told her to keep the change.

The last of the big spenders?

"Thanks for the dinner, Floyd. Now that I'm working full time at Gordon's for the summer, I'm going to have some money in my pocket too. I don't have any savings because Johnny controlled all of our money. Beside that, you know, it's hard on teachers to not see a paycheck all summer. I'm trying to stretch out my June pay as long as possible."

After we finished eating, Floyd drove us around Marquette Park. We enjoyed the cool lake breezes. The smell of the lake was refreshing. Floyd wanted to park for awhile. I knew what that meant.

"No. I'd love to sit here for a while with you,.. watching the waves roll in,… but it's not dark yet and someone might see us together. I don't want to be seen parking with you. I guess you had better drop me off at the bus stop so I can pretend I just came home by bus, as usual."

What I didn't think about was that I didn't pay any attention to the bus schedule. But Mom did. She knew I was lying when she heard the bus go by, on a half hour schedule, just minutes before or after I came "innocently" into the house. I was glad to be home for the evening.

Chapter Fifteen

Valparaiso, Indiana

"Hi, Mom." She was doing up the dinner dishes. I gave her my apology and alibi about standing her up for dinner. She accepted it and said,

"You look beat! Was it as hot in Gordon's as it has been the last few days?"

"Yes, even worse. Working on and off at Gordon's like I've done the last few years is enough to make anyone determined to get a degree or the training to work someplace else! I'm so grateful to you and Dad for sending me down to I.U. for a degree in education. Even if my emergency teaching certificate is only a temporary one, until I pick up a few more credits."

"Well, you're getting there. First it was *Abnormal Psychology* at the extension in downtown Gary and now it's *Music for the Classroom* at Valparaiso University."

"And I'm also taking *Children's Literature* by correspondence, because I can't find it at any of the schools nearby. But it's fun, and by fall when the new school year begins, I'll be able to draw a full salary as a credentialed teacher.

"That will be a lot better. We're so proud of you for being able to start teaching after only three years in college, and for hanging in there until you picked up these few credits.

"Here, I saved a piece of pie for you. Do you want it now?"

"Did I hear someone say 'pie'?" Bert had heard that magic word and came into the kitchen to join us. We sat down at the table and waited for Mom to serve us, and herself.

Bert was working for the summer in the personnel department in the steel mills. I found it was hard to believe that she was making more than a beginning teacher makes. She was considering not going back to school but to take a lucrative raise and a new job if she agreed to stay with the mills in the fall. Bert joined in on the conversation.

"Let's see, tomorrow you'll spend most of the day busing over and back to that class in Valpo, won't you?"

"Yeh, it's a long haul but I don't mind so much. Valparaiso is such a pretty little town. I enjoy walking around in it on my way to class and then back to the bus station."

Mom just sat there with her coffee and listened to her two girls visit.

Bert wanted to know what my schedule was for the week.

"It really worked out well with Gordon's. There it's the usual Monday and Thursday nights from 5:00 to 9:00 (and secretive rides home at night with Floyd!) and all day from 9:00 to 5:00 on Wednesdays and Saturdays. Then I go to school on Mondays, Wednesdays and Fridays. In between I work on that *Kid's Lit* correspondence course so I can get it finished before September rolls around."

"You sure don't let any grass grow under your feet, do you?"

"No, that's what makes life exciting."

But fitting time in to seeing Floyd on the sly really complicates things.

"And, without a car, you get to Valpo by bus? That really took some figuring out!"

"Well, that's another story in itself. I take a city bus to downtown Gary and walk to the Greyhound Station. There I catch one of their buses to Valpo, about 20 miles away. I'm lucky because it arrives just in time for me to walk a mile or two to the campus and get there for my 10:00 o'clock class. It lasts 2 hours but the next Greyhound doesn't leave for Gary until 2:30.

"So, what do you do in the meantime? Read?"

"That's the best time of all. I enjoy that beautiful old town so much that I take a different route back to the station every day. The city sits on a high ridge so that the breezes are cool. I don't think the fact that the ridge is a big GLACIAL moraine has anything to do with it being cool!"

Bert snickered and Mom looked puzzled at my attempt to be funny. Bert explained it to Mom.

"You know, a <u>glacial</u> moraine would be icy and breezes over it should be cool, shouldn't they?" We all laughed together. Then I continued,

"On my walks on Main Street going uphill I get to the courthouse square, I have time to really study the exteriors and yards of those lovely old mansions that were built in the late 19th century. The 'Gay Nineties'? I look for original wavy hand-blown glass window panes and hand carved front doors. And lace curtains. And beautiful old wrought iron fences. And fine gardens filled with neatly trimmed shrubbery and summer flowers."

"And I'll bet you 'take time to smell the roses', too!"

"My sister knows me, doesn't she? Just last week I found the old opera house dated 1892, still charming and in good repair. It was built as a memorial to soldiers of the Civil War. I like to imagine the fine gentlemen and their ladies pulling up to the opera house in their horse-drawn carriages. They are all decked out in their elegant clothes, all satin and velvet, and furs in the wintertime. Such fun!"

Mom joined in with, "Valparaiso is such an old, elegant town, the streets all lined with ancient elm trees. When I was young the University law school there was known as 'the Poor Man's Harvard."

"Mom, you wouldn't know the campus today. It's grown so. But still really beautiful. I just love college campuses."

Bert added, "And you love being on one as a student, don't you?"

"I sure do. It's so exciting. But one of the funniest sights is in town on my walks is when I get close to the square. Every afternoon some of the old men can be seen shuffling up the streets toward the

Greyhound Station. By 2:00 about 10 or 15 of them have assembled there on the wooden chairs in the waiting room. That's one of the few places in the whole town where they have television. The men are visiting and waiting for the pretty girl in short-shorts to come on the T.V. She demonstrates how we should do her daily exercises with her. Not much visiting between the old men goes on then! As soon as that program is over they laboriously get themselves up and out of their chairs and start ambling home, continuing to get their constitutional walks for the day.

"About that time my bus comes and I reverse the route I took in the morning. It takes me almost all day."

And then my mind wanders. *I don't get to see Floyd because he is working. He can't even help me out on transportation. Oh, well. Sometimes I stay downtown until he gets off work and we have dinner together. I have various alibis for Mom to cover up why I'm skipping dinner at home. I hope she never gets wise about how I am lying to her. But back to Mom and Bert...*

"That was really good pie, Mom. It sure hit the spot... Well, if you two will excuse me, I have some studying to do. I'll see you in the morning."

They replied with their own 'Good Night' and I walked back to the bedroom that Bert and I shared, as usual.

Chapter Sixteen

The Confrontation

Fall, 1951

By September, 1951, I was still living at home in my old bedroom. Dad and Mom had welcomed me into their loving arms. None of us realized how many times I would test this evidence of their love in the next few years.

I began my second year of teaching, again in a fourth grade at Glen Park School. The kids were great. Televisions had been available for several years but they had been too expensive for the average family. Finally, in 1951 the prices began to come down. Many people started getting TVs in their homes. I thought that I could tell which families had new TV's because their children got groggy or even fell asleep if we had a quiet reading or study period around 10:00 AM!

My divorce from Johnny Lockhart became finalized that fall and I felt released to begin dating Floyd openly. It was time to introduce him to my parents.

Floyd came. I introduced him.

"Mom and Dad, I want you to meet Floyd Dubois, the fellow I have been dating. He's coming here to pick me up this Friday evening. I hope you like him."

We all sat formally in the living room. My parents were unusually reserved. Not at all friendly and hospitable. It seemed that all of their parental instincts came to the fore. They were already reacting in a very negative manner.

Dad asked the usual questions.

"Well, Floyd, where do you live? In what part of town?"

Floyd answered with respect, "I live with my dad on the west side."

"You graduated from which high school? Horace Mann?"

"Yes, that's right. I graduated two years before Barbara did."

Mom and I sat quietly with our hands in our laps. I crossed and then uncrossed my legs, trying to get comfortable. I patted down my hair and put on a tentative smile.

"Do you have a job?"

"I work for my Dad and take classes at the extension."

"And your work? What kind of business is your father in?"

Why is Dad grilling poor Floyd like this? Isn't there a kinder way of getting to know each other?

"My dad is a contractor and builds houses all over town."

"So, you're a college student but you are about two years older than Barbara. Don't you have a degree yet? What is your major?"

"I want to go into social work and be a psychologist."

'But do you have a major?"

'No, sir. I just pick up classes that I think will be interesting to me."

Wow! I didn't know that! I never questioned him as to how much schooling he had! He always seemed to be such a sincere student.

"And where did you two first meet?"

"We met in a class at Indiana University Extension last winter."

Oh, no! Why did he tell them that? Now they know we met before I left Johnny! Now we're really in for it!

Floyd continued, "The class was called *Abnormal Psychology*, and we both enjoyed it very much. We've been very good friends ever since."

Why is he re-emphasizing it? I think he's deliberately digging my hole deeper and deeper. Why is he deliberately setting us up for criticism?

There was a long silence. It was as though Dad didn't have any more to say and surely Mom would never speak up. I fidgeted with my watch and finally said,

"Well, I guess it is time for us to leave. Ah…, we're going to a movie."

Everyone stood up. Floyd formally shook hands with my parents, saying goodbye, and Dad said,

"We're glad to have finally met you, Floyd."

They knew all of the time! I hadn't fooled them one bit! All of that lying for nothing! I wanted so much to maintain a good reputation and Floyd blew it, just like that! Why did he do it? They'll never warm up to him now.

I couldn't wait to get out of there. As soon as we got into Floyd's car I broke down and started crying. He roared backward out of the driveway, tires squealing, and headed toward the drive-in movie theater. I dug a handkerchief out of my purse, blew my nose and tried to stop crying, so I could talk. He looked at me with scorn.

"Floyd, why in the world did you tell them that we knew each other while I was married to Johnny?

"There's no harm in that. Can't someone have other friends even though married?"

"Of course," I sniffled despite my hankie. "But they are already suspicious about our relationship. You can't expect them to like you if they think you broke up my marriage."

"Look, Bonnie. I don't care what your folks think. I'm free, not beholden to them in any way. They might as well know right now, that I'm not bound by their rules."

"But they are my parents. Don't you want them to accept you? Doesn't that mean anything to you?"

"The sooner you break the stranglehold they have on you, the better. You're an adult now and it's time to start acting like one."

"But I love my folks. Do you think that is childish? Is that why you and your dad don't get along? You don't love him?"

"That has nothing to do with it. I'm honest about my beliefs and I stand by them. I am not paying homage to any hide-bound religious or cultural restraints and I don't expect you to either!"

What's going on here? Am I really too controlled by my parents and their moral standards? Is that why I resist them and their advice? I want to be independent? But they won't let me? ….. Actually, I'm not getting anywhere in this discussion with Floyd. I'll just let it ride for awhile.

Chapter Seventeen

The Explosion

Floyd and I started dating even more frequently. I only showed up for dinner about half of the time, but didn't tell Mom I wouldn't be there. Floyd brought me home far too late for someone who had to teach the next day. Mom and Dad were getting more and more critical of him and of my behavior with him.

Several months later, Mom and Dad told me they wanted to talk to Floyd when he picked me up, again on a Friday night. I had no idea how I could handle what I knew was going to be a very explosive situation. Dad was always the diplomat but I knew he was in no mood for diplomacy this night. When Floyd arrived I asked him to come in and I sat next to him on the couch. Mom and Dad sat in the fireside chairs on the opposite side of the living room. Floyd reached for my hand to pat it and hold it. Perhaps he was giving reassurance to me.

Or was he wanting to indicate possession of me?

When I saw Mom stiffen up and frown, I withdrew my hand.

Dad started out with, "Floyd, we are very concerned about the hours you two are keeping and…"

"Why is that any concern of yours?"

"Because Barbara is our daughter and we are very worried about her. We are very worried about the influence you seem to have on her."

"She is an adult and if she chooses to spend some of her late evenings with me, there is nothing you can do about it!"

"But she is living in our home and we have decent rules to be obeyed if she is to continue to live under our roof!"

"Stop it, you two." I screamed. "Why are you talking about me like this as though I don't even exist? I'm not going to listen to either one of you!"

I put my hands over my ears and ran sobbing back to my bedroom. I threw myself on my bed and cried. But no one came back to console me or try to make me feel better, so I sat up and tried to hear what was going on in the living room. I heard Floyd shout,

"That sir, is none of your business."

And Mom was murmuring over and over, "Now, Gilbert, take it easy," and "Slow down, Honey."

I had never heard my dad swear but it sound like he was getting to that point.

I heard Floyd say something in a low, threatening tone and Dad absolutely blew up.

Dad bellowed, "Floyd Dubois, GET OUT OF HERE! Don't you ever dare to set foot on our property again or I'll call the police."

I ran out of the bedroom, threw my arms around Dad's neck and cried, "Oh, Daddy…" but he pushed me aside and said, "And you might as well take this slut with you!"

Mom was sobbing and trying to restrain Dad from slugging Floyd, and I was bawling and trying to push Floyd out the front door. I ran back in to grab my purse, and as I left a second time, I called back,

"I LOVE YOU, DADDY!"

Chapter Eighteen

Independence

As Floyd and I headed towards town we were silent except for Floyd voicing his plans as to where he was taking me.

"Well, I can't take you to Hotel Gary. They won't let you have a room because you don't have any luggage. We'll try a lesser hotel. Maybe they won't be as concerned about their image."

I clenched my teeth. *Well, that's OK about their image, but what does that say about me?*

I had so much running through my mind that I had nothing to say to him. I just hunched over in my seat, drawing my legs and arms to my stomach, as though to protect my innards. Whenever I thought of Dad's uncontrolled anger I started to cry. I didn't blame him for calling me a slut. I knew he didn't mean it.

Was that really where I was heading? I shivered in the cold November night air. I didn't want to think about anything. Just find me a bed somewhere.

Floyd sauntered, and I meekly followed him, into the lobby of a seedy hotel downtown. The air was musky with the stench of stale tobacco smoke. There was a bare light bulb burning over the check-in desk. It seemed that everything else in the room was a dull ancient brown. It was late and the desk clerk looked like we had just awakened him.

"She needs a room for the night."

"Do you have luggage to bring in?" he said to me.

"No"

"I'm sorry ma'am, but I can't let you stay here unless you bring in luggage." He nodded his head sideward toward Floyd and raised his eyebrows.

"No, that's not it! We just had a big fight with my parents and they kicked me out. That's why I don't have any luggage." I began to cry again.

"Honest, it's just for me. He won't be coming up to my room. Please sir, can't you find a room for me?"

"Do your parents know you are coming here tonight? Will there be any trouble with them?"

"No, they have no idea where I am going to end up."

None of us do!

"Well then, I guess I can find something for you," he said in a lazy, insolent manner. "It's against our rules you know. We are a reputable establishment and can't afford any negative publicity."

"I know. I won't cause any problems."

Floyd paid for one night's lodging while I signed the guest register. The clerk gave me the key to my room. I shook hands with Floyd. With an air of finality, I said, "Good night, I'll see you in the morning." I headed for the elevator.

I was numb. I didn't have one ounce of love or passion left for that man who had precipitated such a disastrous split between my parents and me.

When I entered my room a neon sign outside was flashing, flashing. Bus fumes assaulted me as I closed the window. I pulled down the shade. Even then I was very aware of the traffic noise of the city. But that wouldn't bother me after I took off my hearing aids. I turned down the bedding. I didn't even check to see if the sheets were clean. I partially undressed and collapsed on the bed. Trembling, I pulled the covers up over me. I was chilled to the bone and I was exhausted. I tossed and turned for only a few minutes, but then fell into a deep sleep. I was mercifully oblivious, for a while, of all that had bombarded me in the last few weeks.

The next morning, feeling very apologetic, I faced up to calling Mom. I cried as I told her where I had spent the night, by myself. I told her I was going to look for a small apartment just for me. I asked her, "If I find one, may I come out and get my stuff?" She said I could come anytime but that she and Dad never wanted to see Floyd again.

Floyd picked me up. We still didn't have much to say to each other. We looked at the rental ads in the paper. We followed one of them and found a little 2 room apartment on the second floor of a private home. It was fully furnished. I insisted that Floyd pay the deposit and the first and last month's rent. The landlady didn't question our relationship as the hotel clerk did.

We went back out to my parents' house that afternoon. I wouldn't let Floyd pull into the driveway. I made him park on the back street. I trudged up a sandy path on a wooded dune through the city park to the back door.

"Hello! Hello? Anybody home?"

All was silent. Either no one was home or Mom didn't admit she was in her bedroom. She didn't want to see me, either!

Oh, well, I shrugged with relief. *It's for the best right now anyway. I'll stuff my clothes into my suitcases and get out as fast as I can.*

We stored my bulging bags safely in Floyd's car. Next I needed to get my household things out of the basement. Floyd climbed up the path on park property until he was near the back door. I struggled to carry each heavy box up the basement stairs. There on the porch I simply shoved it at him. He stumbled unsteadily down the hill with each box and packed it also into his car. As we drove away with the car stuffed to the roofline, I looked back with deep grief. We stopped for some groceries for my little refrigerator. All I wanted now was to get everything into the apartment and to be left alone.

Later, I looked around at the pile of boxes in my crowded apartment and groaned. *So, this is the independence I've been wanting?*

Well, welcome to heartache all over again. And to being my own boss. And loneliness. And no one to talk to.

I spent the balance of the weekend unpacking and getting the apartment in shape, and getting MYSELF in shape for going back into my classroom on Monday morning.

What a weekend that was! I sure didn't ever want to go through another one like that! Thank God I have my students to concentrate on this morning. I'll be ready for them with a loving smile on my face, and my broken heart out of sight until this evening.

Chapter Nineteen

Counseling, Conflict

SPRING, 1952

"But I just don't understand what's going on with me. I feel like I'm being pulled apart by you two and by Floyd. I just don't know what to do."

My folks and I were sitting around the kitchen table and talking, talking, talking. Just like before, up until the time I married Johnny. After the big blow-up with Floyd they welcomed me to come to visit whenever I wanted.

"Just don't bring Floyd along with you."

"Bobbie, I guess we can't advise you," Dad said. "It's obvious you are not going to quit seeing Floyd. We feel he is leading you into a total disaster. We absolutely cannot stand him. Our feelings are dead set against him."

"Your dad and I think he is at the root of all of your trouble, ever since you met him. We don't understand this grip he seems to have on you."

"It's not a grip. I am just so intrigued by him. He is everything Johnny wasn't. He's so intelligent. I find him challenging and very exciting."

"That may well be. But your mother and I have talked this over. We think you need to discuss this with someone who is neutral, someone who can look at your situation in an impartial manner."

There was a pause. Mom took a deep breath, reached for my hand to hold it. She leaned toward me to emphasize the seriousness of what she had to say.

"Bobbie, Dear, how about going to a psychiatrist or psychologist for counseling?"

"I'm that bad off, huh?"

I scratched my head and stalled while thinking that through.

"Your mom and I are thinking you might go to Dr. Fitzgerald from church. He's well known in the area and has his office right down on Lake Street."

"No way! I can't go to anyone from around here! What if someone sees me going into his office? I know about psychological counseling, but others will think I'm crazy, or something! Besides, everyone knows he's doing a lousy job raising his own kids." After another pause I said,

"OK, I can do it. I'll call Dr. Jacob, my former psychology prof. He has a private practice and his office is downtown in the bank building. I know he'll see me." I wondered, was my willingness to take their advice for a change, a measure of my desperation?

Dr. Jacob

I made the promised phone call.

"Dr. Jacob? I'm Barbara Conway. I'm a former student of yours. My friend, Floyd Dubois and I were in your Abnormal Psychology class at I.U. Extension. I guess I need some counseling. Could I make an appointment to come in and talk with you…. soon?"

He had time for me. I agreed to a late afternoon time so that I could see him after school. I anxiously waited for the day to arrive. I was very busy planning all of the things I was going to tell him.

When the afternoon finally arrived, I found his office. As I sat there waiting, I had a growing sense of panic. Could I really be as honest with him as I needed to be if I was going to get any help? I was very uncomfortable but I silently vowed that I would try to be totally transparent, even if it hurt.

Dr. Jacob greeted me, shook my hand, and motioned to his inner sanctum. I entered and the only place for me to sit was the long brown leather couch that I knew I was supposed to recline on. Just like in the movies!

He closed the door behind him. I didn't lie down, however. I perched on the edge of the couch. It would soon be my time to spill my guts to him. I knew he wouldn't put it that way but that was the way I felt about it!

I have important things to talk to him about, questions to be answered, and things to explain. I'm coming here to learn to find out why or how I get myself into such a mess with Floyd and my folks, _and what I should do about it._

But I was wrong. It wasn't to be done my way.

"Please lie down, Barbara, and try to relax."

But I feel so awkward and vulnerable. How does he know I'm all wound up inside? …… I guess that's his job… and I guess it's not really unusual, especially at the first session.

So, I did as I was told. I tried to lie on my side so I could see his face. The couch was very hard and stiff and I didn't have a pillow to prop my head on. I was forced to lay flat on my back and stare at the ceiling. I crossed my feet at the ankles and folded my hands over my stomach. And I waited…..

"Well, now, didn't you tell me on the phone that you and your friend Floyd Dubois were in my Abnormal Psychology class a little more than a year ago?"

"Yes, that is where we first met." Since I couldn't see him I felt like I was talking to a spooky shadow over in the corner of the room.

"I remember Floyd very well. But, correct me if I'm wrong. I recognize your face but your last name wasn't Conway then?"

"No, I was married but that only lasted about nine months Last spring, after I met Floyd, I left my husband and filed for a divorce. It was finalized last fall and I took back my maiden name."

"Why have you come to me?"

"You are the only counselor that I know. I need some neutral advice for helping me sort out a big jam that I've gotten myself into."

"Well, why don't you just let go and tell me about it?"

Let it all hang out? OK, here I go.

"I've been dating Floyd after my divorce but my folks can't stand him. He had a big fight with my dad. They say they are very worried about me because I don't want to break up with Floyd or to take their advice. They suggested that I get some counseling from a neutral source, so here I am."

"So, you've been having trouble with your parents over your dating? When do you think that first started? Were they critical only of Floyd?"

"No, they've never approved of anyone I dated. Way back in high school, I started going steady with my first boyfriend against my folks' advice. I didn't think I could attract another guy. I guess I masked my insecurities by agreeing to go steady rather than playing the field. He really was a great guy and we had a lot of fun together. I thought that girls who didn't settle down with one boyfriend at a time were 'loose' or immoral."

"How long did you go steady?"

"For two and a half years in high school and on and off all the way through college."

"Did you become intimate?"

"Well. We....I mean, I...." *I want to get out of here! He makes me feel so intimidated. Better face it and get it over with.*

"Yes. I... I always felt very guilty about it. I prayed and prayed and made promises to God, but I wasn't willing to stop us whenever we started to neck. We were so much in love. In addition to my sense of guilt, I was deathly afraid of getting pregnant. Finally I quit praying for the strength to quit having sex with Johnny. Every month while I was sitting on the stool in the bathroom, anxiously waiting for my period to start, I even tried to bargain with God. I promised that if He would keep me from getting pregnant now, I'd never ask for children of my own! (see also: "Childlessness" stories in Notebook # 6, "Recalling, The Middle Years")

Johnny wanted so very much to get married right out of high school but I didn't even consider it. I insisted that we wait to get married until after I graduated from Indiana University and could start teaching. When that time came around, we still loved each other, but I felt compelled to marry him rather than call the wedding off at the last minute. I didn't want to embarrass our parents or hurt him."

"Why were you questioning this?"

"My parents had argued against my dating and marrying Johnny from the beginning because our backgrounds and our aspirations in life were so different. Finally I understood how that might cause serious problems in a marriage."

"And did it?"

"Yes. Johnny didn't look at my teaching as a career. I think he felt intimidated by it. When I began comparing Johnny with Floyd… Well, this last year has been straight out of Hell. I've been thinking and behaving in a way that I never imagined would be me. Some of the time I was so obviously 'out of character', it was as though I was living two different lives. In one of them, I was a respectable school teacher. In the other, even though I was married, I was excited with having coffee with Floyd after class. I knew this innocent appearing sociability was actually infidelity on my part. Floyd seemed to be everything great that Johnny wasn't. We seemed to have much more in common than Johnny and I could ever have. Then, after asking Johnny for a divorce, I began secretly dating Floyd. Mom and Dad welcomed me back home and I moved back into my old bedroom."

"They didn't know about Floyd at that time?"

"No. When I finally introduced Floyd to them, after my divorce, I believe all of their instincts as my parents came out. They forcefully objected to him as even my friend and most especially as a suitor. I moved out after Floyd had a big fight with my dad. I didn't know then that Floyd threatened Dad with a gun and that during World War II Floyd was given a psychological discharge from the army!... I rented a small apartment by myself for a few months, but now I'm living back home again."

"Do you think your interest in Floyd had anything to do with your decision to divorce Johnny?"

In a much softer voice, I admitted,

"Yes, I know it did. Johnny always loved me. He was lots of fun and a wonderful boyfriend in high school." At this point tears of regret began coursing down my cheeks. "Johnny was stable, a good man. He always treated me well and would have made a great father for our children....,"

After a long pause I choked up with sobs and whispered, "and I ended up hurting him very, very much, after all." In a flash of amazement and regret, I added, "But I lost sight of all his good qualities after I met Floyd."

"Why do you think you were vulnerable to Floyd's influence?"

I said, "I have no idea. "

That's your job. To listen to every thing I can remember about something and then tell me why or what to do next.

"Well, that's something you might think about for our next session, if you feel we should continue working together."

I told Dr. Jacob that I wanted to hang in there with him. We discussed time and fees. I felt it was a good decision and I committed myself to seeing him the following week, and as long as we both felt our sessions were fruitful. I said goodbye and headed for the bus.

Chapter Twenty

Counseling, Religion

The following week I perched on the edge of that dark brown leather reclining couch, this time just to express defiance. At Doctor Jacob's 'suggestion', I submitted and lay down on the couch anyway. Dr. Jacob, my professor, now psychologist, took his seat beside my head, where I couldn't make eye contact or watch him take notes.

This really makes me squirm. For all I know, he might be just picking at his fingernails (or his nose!) in boredom. But I don't want eye contact with him anyway. He can hypnotize people. I'm never going to let anyone use that on me (Little did I know!).

He took up the session from where we left off the last time.

"Barbara, we were trying to figure out why you were so vulnerable to Floyd's influence. How would you sum up your feelings about your dating experiences until you married Johnny?"

Well, now is the time to be as honest as I possibly can, even if it hurts. Otherwise I can't expect him to help me, can I?

"From the time I started dating in high school I was at odds with my parents on the subject of my dating. In college I dated a non-Christian, a Hindu, no less, and considered marrying him. Mom and Dad were very worried. After I broke up with him, at their insistence, I dated several other college students for awhile but Mom and Dad objected to almost every man I brought home for them to meet. They didn't think Johnny, my high school sweetheart, would be a good choice as a husband. I guess they just wanted the best for me. They wanted me to be perfect and for my husband to be likewise."

I tried to swallow some non-existent saliva and struggled with saying,

"Now, I…I'm afraid I'm no better than other young women that I've criticized most of my life."

"Criticized? What about?"

"Well, morality and, I guess, sexual purity, and stuff like that."

Now, I don't even want eye contact with my doctor. It is easier to talk about embarrassing things this way. Boy, is this tough! What will he ask next?

"I've been thinking about our last session and a reference you made to God. Are you aware of any conflicts in your religious convictions?"

Now, where does that come from? What does religion have to do with anything?

But I said, "Well, I felt kinda at loose ends as to religion ever since I entered high school."

Where's he going with this?

"I was a freshman when we moved into a new community and started attending a new church there instead of where I grew up. At the Chapel of the Dunes they didn't seem to have any dogma. …..No, that's not fair. It was there but I wasn't in any mood to recognize any of it as truth."

"Why didn't you accept their doctrine?"

"We kids went to Sunday school every week. My grandmother was devout and everyone in my mother's family followed her. We read our weekly study lessons together every day, just as the adults did. When I was a child, even then, some of what they taught was hard to believe. I knew that God was a loving God, and would protect me from harm, but that was about all. I guess I didn't believe what other churches taught either.

"I just couldn't accept the idea that man here on earth was perfect,

I mean *really* perfect, made in God's image and likeness. Therefore we had no need of medical care, that doctors were unnecessary for our physical well being."

"No medical care?"

"I just didn't believe all that stuff about never going to a doctor. I had horrible earaches every winter, when I was a kid. They were real. That pain wasn't just my imagination or my lack of faith in God. I don't know. Maybe that's just my childish understanding of what I was taught."

"What other conflicts were you aware of concerning church or religion?"

"Well, when I was a young teen-ager I wanted our Sunday School to plan social activities for young people. They didn't recognize the value of them in guiding teenagers in dating and things like that. I went to my girlfriend's social events at her Presbyterian church. I probably soaked up some of their doctrine at the same time. That only increased my rebellion. When we moved, I looked forward to youth activities at our new church. But soon I decided church as more of a social scene for adults, rather than a teaching, or studying, or a learning experience for me. I never went to the youth meetings and parties at the Chapel."

"Why not?"

What does this have to do with Floyd and me?

"I guess I didn't have enough nerve to walk in all by myself as a stranger. I was afraid of being rejected. Many years later I saw how eagerly most church groups embrace the newcomers! When I started dating Johnny, he and his family didn't go to any church. He refused to go with me, so we never became active in the youth activities at The Chapel of the Dunes. I continued to sing in the adult choir and go to church without him."

"You seemed to be much more concerned about social activities than religion itself, yet you didn't participate in church with other young people when you had a chance. Am I right?"

"Yes, and the sermons… I didn't have a learner's attitude. So I just kept my mouth shut and didn't question things out loud that conflicted with my "so called" faith. I listened to the Bible stories from the pulpit. I accepted some of them as mostly true. But I didn't even know that Christians have that name because they believe in Jesus Christ as God, part of the Trinity. I didn't want to put up with any spiritual stuff. None of that applied to me. I had my fill of reading daily lessons from the Bible. That was something that only old ladies like my grandma and mother did.

"I guess I used the Chapel of the Dunes to support my reputation, because 'All good people go to church someplace, don't they?' Above all, I was a Good Girl who loved God, and my family and I were admirable and respectable, morally without fault."

"Do you think any of this disillusionment affected your behavior?"

"When I entered the later teen years I rebelled against much of my early training as being too idealistic. There were times when I felt I…I was out of fellowship with God. I felt I was unworthy before God. I guess that carried over to insecurity in dating. I got so that I doubted the validity of some biblical commands concerning sex and abstinence. I thought they were unrealistic. I was really torn and very defiant, even against some of our cultural mores. I knew the Ten Commandments. I knew I was on a path of disobedience."

"Very good," he said as he released me from that session. "Here's something for you to consider for next time. Many times the loss of religious faith results in a destructive life style. I want you to consider how this might relate to your life."

I was on my way home. On the bus after my counseling session, my present predicament caught up with me. I knew that what Dr. Jacob suggested really could apply to me.

But for the time being, I stopped trying to reason out why I was going through this moral crisis. My thoughts turned to how Grandma used to say, 'Get thee behind me, Satan," (*1) when she was tempted to help us finish up the last slice of her great homemade cherry and gooseberry pie.

Maybe she really did believe that the devil exists and that he tempts us. I don't remember hearing anything about him in Sunday school. But what is that verse about how Satan goes around seeking whom he can devour? (*2) And why did I think of that now? Does it have anything to do with what was going on between Floyd and me?

*1- "But He turned and said to Peter, "Get behind Me, Satan. You are a stumbling block to Me; for you are not setting your mind on God's interests; but on man's."(Matt.16: 23. ---NAS)

*2- "Be of sober spirit, be on the alert. Your adversary, the devil, prowls about like a lion, seeking someone to devour. But resist him, firm in your faith..."

(I Pet. 5: 8, 9. ---NAS)

Part Three

Impaled...
The Escape

Chapter Twenty-one

Counseling, Moving

During the next few sessions Dr. Jacob led me to admit that with Floyd, I was on my way to a personal disaster.

Just before school let out for the summer, I followed Dr. Jacob's suggestion to find out if Mom and Dad would let me move back home again. Of course, they welcomed me back, for the third time!

After several more sessions of questioning me and hearing me out, Dr. Jacob recommended that I move away from both my parents and Floyd in order to relieve the pressure. That made good sense to me and, in answer to my call to travel and see the rest of the world, I decided to look for a teaching job along the coast of Washington or Oregon. When I told him that, he said that he didn't mean for me to burn all of my bridges behind me. He thought that a short move away would have been better, but my mind was made up. I wanted to be as far away from Floyd Dubois as possible.

Mom and I wrote what we thought would be an effective job inquiry. I sent out 27 letters to school districts all along the coast of Washington and Oregon. I enclosed a letter from my principal of the last two years. It was an excellent recommendation as a teacher. I was very proud of it because I knew it was a testimony as to how I was able to function in the classroom despite all that was going on in my private life.

When the school superintendent of Aberdeen, Washington called long distance to offer me a job on the spot, I was so flattered. I didn't realize that it was only a reflection of the teacher shortage that existed all during and after World War II until war veterans completed their schooling and began to move into the classrooms. I didn't wait to see if any other offers would be better. I accepted a third grade position right then even if I wasn't wild about third grade. The next day other offers started arriving by special delivery and later by regular mail. I eventually was offered jobs in response to all of my 27 letters! That's what I got for not doing adequate research!

Mom and Dad offered to drive me out to Washington, along with Bert and Milt. John was in the Navy and overseas. In August we packed my belongings into a two wheeled trailer. I said a last, final goodbye to Floyd with a profound sense of relief. In high spirits the five of us set off on a family trip of a lifetime.

Packing Up, Westward, HO! 1952
Dad, Bert, Mom

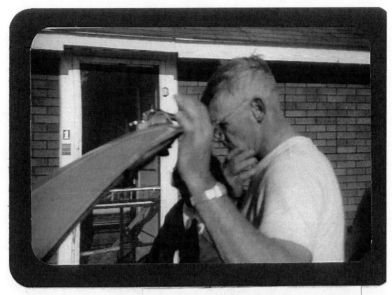

"Where you gonna put it all, Daddy?"

"Hey, we're almost there!"

Enjoying Our National Parks

Camping in Black Hills National Park

Our forest campground in Yellowstone National Par.

Chapter Twenty-Two

Westward, Ho!

We were all happy and excited we began our first trip to the west coast. We traveled in a bright red station wagon. We pulled a small two wheel trailer that carried all of my moving 'stuff' in an army surplus foot locker.

Dad built a raised platform floor in the back of the station wagon so we could put suitcases under it. Mom and Dad put their air mattresses and sleeping bags on top of it and slept there. Bert and Milt slept in a small tent that had enough room for me too, but I liked to fall asleep on my cot out under the stars and feel the dew on my face when I awakened the next morning.

The car was stuffed to the gills with the five of us; Mom, Dad, Bert, Milt, and me, along with sleeping bags, air mattresses, and 2 wooden orange crates filled with pots and dishes in one and groceries in the other. The rack on the roof carried our tent, a few cots, and luggage. The foot locker was filled with my things that I thought were essential for moving and teaching 2,000 miles away from home. Over the trailer we tied down an old khaki army blanket. We laughed at ourselves and said we looked like a band of gypsies who were just making off with a stolen, brand-new, pretty, red station-wagon!

It was a great trip. We had a chance to restore our sense of family unity. I was part of the family again and I loved all of them very much. My sister Bert was eighteen and I was twenty three. It was the first time in our lives that we enjoyed each other as equals rather than as competitors. Then, of course, we all missed John. John and I had a special bond. We were the only ones in the family who had red hair! He couldn't make the trip with us because, at age seventeen, he enlisted in the Navy right out of high school. He was probably somewhere out on the Pacific heading toward Japan. And then, all three of us older kids treasured our youngest brother most of all. Milt was eleven years old and we were very proud of him.

The trip out west was even more wonderful because I was leaving Floyd behind and all that moral tumult that he had caused. I could start all over again in a new life that I could be proud of. I was also fulfilling my dreams of travel.

We took our time on our first trip to the Northwest, camping along the way in state and national parks. As we broke camp each morning, Mom and Bert and I packed everything up as Dad and fellow drivers gathered around maps spread out on the hood of a car. They discussed how to get to the next park and what to see on the way. Then Dad put everything away in the back of the station wagon and in the rack on top of the car, and we were off!

Late one afternoon as we were cruising through campgrounds looking for a space that suited our fancy, we were puzzled at an 11 year-old's criteria as to where to settle, because Milt frequently asked Dad to go on and try the next campground. We were amused when we found out that he was looking for the car of the boy that he had played with the previous night.

In one of the mountainous forest campgrounds the ranger assured us that we could drink the water from the creek. That sounded like a lot of fun so we sent Milt down to the creek with the old aluminum milk can that we had used all of my life. It held a gallon of milk, had a tight lid and a strong bail or handle. When I was a child Mom and Dad drove out to a farm not far away and bought pail full of milk every two or three days. This was less expensive than having it delivered from the dairy.

When Mom and we kids went camping on the banks of the Tippecanoe River in Indiana with Aunt Mary and our cousins, every day Dot and Dick and I, as the oldest ones, got up on the Nickel Plate railroad tracks and walked to the farm of the farmer who owned the riverbank pasture where we were camping. We bought milk from him and on the way home swung the pail between us. If it had been cream, we would have made butter before we got back to camp!

That old milk pail had more than its share of dings and dents and we treasured it greatly as a relic from our past. After too long getting the water from the creek, Milt came back looking downcast, empty handed, and his clothes were all wet. He explained that the bank of the creek was undercut and there was a small cliff about three feet high and that he couldn't really get down to the water to fill the can. So he tied a rope onto the bail and lowered the can into the swiftly moving water. The rope came untied, the can got away and it went rolling and bumping over the rocks in the shallow water. In panic, he jumped in after it, yelling for help as he raced downstream with it, trying to catch it. Other kids jumped in too, trying to help but the water was too swift and it got away from them. Milt was one sad boy. He had lost our poor old milk can and he was freezing from the icy mountain water in the creek.

Lo and behold, the next morning as we were getting packed up to hit the road again, someone asked us if this pail was ours! Some boys found it hung up in some rocks that they said was about a mile downstream and it had been passed up from one campground to the next looking for its owner. So, then our milk pail had some new unique dents in it and another story we loved to tell about it.

97

Chapter Twenty-three

Seattle, Washington

ℒATE SUMMER, 1952

We had a wonderful trip across the northern part of our country from Lake Michigan to Seattle. I was feeling great, so lighthearted in my new-found freedom. As a family, our love had triumphed over conflict. We were again having fun together, with the pain of the past deliberately put behind us.

As Dad pulled into Seattle, we all started talking at once. We sounded more like a bunch of kids let out for recess rather than four adults and a younger brother.

I couldn't contain my surprise.

"Oh, golly! How beautiful! Just look at how tall those hills are! And so green!"

We were sniffing at the fresh ocean breezes. Mom said,

"Can you smell the ocean? Salt water smells different than Lake Michigan, doesn't it?"

"Hey, look at all the boats in the water!"

"Milt, when they're that big, we call them ships."

"Yes, teacher!"

"I can't believe this hill. It's so steep! Each cross street makes a level step and we then climb up to the next one."

"It's like a 'rolley coaster' trudging up to the sky!"

"Yeh, I can't wait until we come back down!"

"If we come back down fast enough, I'll bet our stomachs will drop like they do in an elevator!"

"Go faster, Daddy!"

"Now, Gilbert, take it easy. Don't get carried away!"

We gawked like country bumpkins coming into the city for the first time. Flatlanders that we were, we were all yapping at once in our amazement at the hills of Seattle. On our trip "Out West" we had been thrilled with the mountains, the deep valleys and the waterfalls. We teased Dad. We said he had taken from three to five pictures of every waterfall between Lake Michigan and the Pacific Ocean! Now we added Seattle to our list of wonders.

Mom, the practical one, broke into our excited chatter with a suggestion that we all thought was great.

"Gilbert, how about skipping a campground for tonight? Let's find a motel and enjoy Seattle for a day or two."

"Yeh, Daddy. Bert and I need to wash our hair and clean up now that we're back in civilization."

"Well, we all need good baths, I guess. And so does the car. It's a mess from those dusty campground roads. OK, Dorothy, if you think we can afford it. Let's go ahead and splurge. First one to see a motel on our side of the street, let out a yell and I'll stop there!"

"Your dad and I will look over the rooms to see if they are clean and Dad will find out how much the rooms run out here on the coast."

The first motel we pulled into was satisfactory after Mom pulled down the sheets to see if they were clean. She always had a fear of finding bed bugs like she did when we were traveling in Virginia before Bert was born.

As Milt looked over the room, he said,

"Yippee! I get to take a long hot bath in a real bathtub instead of washing from a bucket set on a picnic table, or a shower in the men's washhouse!"

"Bobbie, we'll get two rooms with a double bed in each one. Milt can sleep on a cot in Dad's and my room. You and Bert can have one room all to yourselves and share the double bed just like you do at home. How does that sound?"

"That sounds great."

Dad and Milt washed the car with our bucket and a sponge while Mom lay down in their room for a little nap.

Bert claimed the tub first because she said she had to wash her hair. I said,

"While you do that, I'll repack our suitcases, and maybe wash out some underwear. I guess, if we are going to go out on the town tonight, I need to find something for us to wear other than our traveling shorts and tee shirts. I think I'll just take a sponge bath at the sink. I want time later this evening to soak a bit before going to bed. I need to get myself looking presentable if I intend to look for a room-and-board when we get to Aberdeen tomorrow."

Dad thought that we should celebrate our arrival on the West Coast by finding some fresh seafood for dinner. The man in the motel office recommended "Ivar's", down on the waterfront.

We were spellbound as we followed the directions down to the bay. Darkness had fallen. This time we were speechless. We couldn't believe our eyes. We thought it was a veritable fairyland, in the original sense of the word, because of all of the city lights at night. They glowed and twinkled all around us: up the hills to the stars and down the slopes to the water. All across the rippling water of Elliot Bay, the lights of West Seattle were reflected just for us. They looked like shimmering stars or the little diamonds darting from sparklers on the Fourth of July. It was magical. We had never seen city lights on hills and reflected on water before. Our cities in the Midwest were always flat or only had small rolling hills. We were simply captivated by seeing so many lights all at once. We agreed to call it "Sparkletown" forever more. We were thoroughly enchanted. Despite the heartache and agony that shortly was to take place for me in Seattle, it always remained one of the most beautiful and beloved cities that I had ever known. I knew I would always think of it as my own shining city on the hills.

Our seafood was excellent. Such a treat for landlubber Hoosiers! Afterward Dad entertained us by singing and cruising around the city looking for steep hills where we could test the speed limit. He made it seem like we were going on carnival rides when we were young. Finally, the travel and excitement of the day caught up with us. We found our motel and flopped into our beds. I decided to take my tub bath in the morning.

HEADING SOUTH

After gallivanting all over Seattle the night before, we awakened early and had to come back down to earth. I enjoyed my tub bath, washed my hair, and put it up in pin curls to dry on the way south. I put on my navy blue polka dot dress again that had become my uniform. (I hand-washed it frequently on the trip.) It was fine for traveling because it was a polyester knit jersey that didn't wrinkle and always looked neat. I wore nylon hose and navy sandals just like in the city the night before, instead of my usual camper's bobby socks and tennis shoes. We were going to drive down along the eastern shore of Puget Sound and then west to Aberdeen, Washington. I was excited about seeing what my new town was like, the school where I would be teaching and about finding a place to live.

On the way, we stopped in Olympia, the state capitol, to see Mom's Cousin Angie. She was expecting us to drop by on our way through town. They knew each other as girls before Cousin Angie's family moved from Indiana to Texas. They hadn't seen each other since then.

Cousin Angie's son was there, too. Clarence seemed to be maybe 15 years older than I, but we were of the same generation. We all enjoyed hearing him talk about his job as a lumber jack for Weyerhaeuser Lumber. He promised me that some weekend soon he would take me, and any friend, deep into the Olympic National Forest. We'd go all the way in, past several older lumber camps to the very end of the road where they were currently cutting timber. He'd tell me all about the lumber business from a lumber company's viewpoint rather than from a politician's stance on forest conservation. Now that was what I called a real, authentic adventure in getting acquainted with the West Coast! I could hardly wait.

Chapter 24

Aberdeen, Washington

On the road again, we took the cutoff from the highway and headed west through Hoquiam to Aberdeen. We followed the Lower Chehalis River to where it empties into Gray's Harbor. When we crossed Indian Creek, we were within a few blocks of the business district of Aberdeen. As we drove west down the main street, we saw the saw mills on the waterfront with hundreds of logs soaking in the wide river mouth and contained by long floating booms. A short business district was only five or six blocks long. That was a much smaller town than I had anticipated.

We decided to locate my school so that I could find a place to rent nearby, since I had no car and would need to walk to work. Dad found A.J. West Elementary School easily. The door was unlocked so I left the family to wait in the car and I went into the office. There I met the principal, Mr. Shipley. As we were getting acquainted, I told him about my need for a nearby room and board. He told me about a friend who was looking for a boarder just a few blocks away. He called Mrs. Welch and got permission to send us right over.

We drove up and stopped in front of a white bungalow with a wide porch across the front of it. Everything was so sparkling and green. The grass was freshly mown and a hedge of gorgeous roses formed a boundary along one side of the small lot. I walked up onto the porch and rang the door bell.

An attractive older woman answered the bell.

"Good afternoon, Mrs. Welch. I'm Barbara Conway and Mr. Shipley sent me over to see you."

"I'm glad to meet you. He said you were going to be teaching here and that you were new to our area. Won't you come in?"

"Yes, thank you. Actually, I'm brand new to the whole West Coast. I'll be teaching third grade over at A.J. West. I'm looking for board and room within walking distance of the school since I don't have a car."

"Well, come along and see the room. You can have the front bedroom which is larger and I'll take the rear one. We'll need to share the bathroom."

"That's OK with me. Oh, this room is great. It even has a good sized closet."

"Of course, you'll have free range of the whole house, including the kitchen. We'll share chores like doing dishes and dusting and things like that."

"That's just fine. Would you like to meet my family? They're waiting out in the car. I'd like Mom and Dad to see the room too."

"Certainly. Ask them to come on in."

I called to my folks. They came in, looked at the room, and said it was very pleasant and large enough for me.

Back in the living room, Mrs. Welch explained that her husband died about six months ago and that she wanted someone in the house to visit with because it was so lonely in the evening. I said that I understood. As my family sat in the living room, she took me to the kitchen to talk business. I liked her right away because she was treating me as an adult. I didn't have to get my parents to approve of our financial agreement. She proposed fifty dollars a month and to split the food and utilities evenly between us. That sounded great to me. We informed Mom and Dad and they agreed that it sounded fair, after Dad asked for an estimate as to how much utilities ran each month! That hadn't occurred to me! So much for being independent!

I offered to rent the room. She agreed and said I could move in right away. Dad and Milt lugged the foot locker and some of my clothes into my room. I unloaded the foot locker so that the folks could take it with them. I had already packed so that my camping clothes were in a smaller suitcase. We hadn't finished our western adventure yet. We told Mrs. Welch that we were going Gray's Harbor State Park campground for a few days. School didn't start until after Labor Day. We wanted to go deep sea fishing before the rest of the family headed home.

Her response was, "If you catch enough fish could you leave...? a small one with me, I'll show Barbara how we bake salmon out here."

Mom said, "That sounds like a good idea. We'll be more than willing to share."

We said good bye for a while, and headed for the campground.

Chapter Twenty-five

Deep Sea Fishing

As our last fling together, before my family headed home, we went down to Gray's Harbor and Dad really splurged by buying us passage and renting all of the gear needed for an all day deep sea fishing excursion. It was something none of us would ever forget. The man at the ticket shack suggested that as landlubbers, we should all take Dramamine a half hour before embarking early the next morning.

Fishing Out of Gray's Harbor, Washington
Dad, Mom, Bert, Bobbie, Milt, and our captain

"Keep your pole up, Bert! Point it to the sky!"

Our boat not only bucked from front to back,
It pitched from side to side!

"Oh, no! You're bringing it in by the tail!"

I slept out in the open as usual, totally at ease and unafraid, enjoying the state park campground, the smell of the fresh sea air and the stars overhead on a beautiful clear night. When I woke up the next morning I was puzzled as to why I was cuddled down into my sleeping bag and even my head and face were buried in it. I uncovered my face and felt what seemed to be a very, very light drizzle and my bag was all covered with sparkling tiny droplets of water. I let the moisture "wash" my face for me as I realized that overnight a very heavy fog had moved in off of the water. It was thicker than any fog I had ever seen in the Midwest. I lay there for a long time just enjoying the beauty of it all, until the sun began to come up and dissipate the moisture in the air.

That morning Mom fried bacon and eggs over the kerosene Coleman stove set on a picnic table, and the five of us sat down to a hearty breakfast before our exciting first adventure on the high seas. We obediently took our Dramamine and headed down to the docks.

Our captain was an interesting fellow who spent his winters cutting fern and mushrooms in the Olympic Forest north of us, and his summers taking his fishing boat out for the likes of us. There were two old grizzled fishermen on board also and they immediately opted to sit up on the bow, as far away from us beginners as they could get. As we got under way we were thrilled with the swells that were rolling into the harbor and thought the roller-coaster ride was great fun. The captain assured us that we hadn't seen anything yet, and promised that as soon as we got out at sea, we would not only roll up on the surges and then plunge down into the troughs between the waves, but that we would begin to roll from side to side at the same time!

When we cleared the mouth of the harbor and were in the open sea, his predictions came true. He and the ocean beneath us gave us a fine ride and we squealed with joy and excitement with every toss that the waves threw at us. In the meantime, those two old fishermen who reminded me of our grandpa were leaning over the rail and turning their stomachs inside out! We verbally expressed our sympathy but I knew we 'kids' were secretly gloating just a bit because that Dramamine apparently worked just fine.

Grandpa never recognized Dad as much of a fisherman. Dad was the only man in the family, a son-in-law, of course, who liked to camp but didn't care much about fishing. We were amazed that Dad spent an uncharacteristic 'bundle' to hire a boat and skipper and then rent all of the necessary tackle to take us out fishing on the huge Pacific Ocean! We were especially in awe when the skipper told us that the buoy out there was the last thing between us and Japan. We knew that Dad was counting on taking a great big fish on dry ice back to Indiana and impress all of the relatives, but Grandpa, especially.

Well, we all caught our limit of salmon except for Dad! We just about fell out of the boat laughing when we saw his only catch being reeled in backwards by the tail! He had snagged a sea bass when the fish threw the hook out of its mouth! The captain suggested that we throw it back in but we knew it was good to eat and we weren't too proud to bring it in along with our salmon.

The skipper cleaned our fish for us. He and Dad packed all but two of them in several small wooden boxes that we dubbed coffins, and they packed fresh ice all around and in the fish, rather than dry ice as we had expected. The skipper explained that dry ice would freeze the fish and dry it out. If Dad repacked the fish every night in fresh ice, they would keep all the way back to Indiana since they were heading right back home after leaving me off in Aberdeen. That night at the campground, Mom fried up the sea bass and it was the best fish we had ever eaten! Then Dad packed the icy fish coffins in the one wheel trailer, covered them with layers of newspaper and tied down over it the old khaki-colored heavy wool army blanket that I had used over my sleeping bag on very cold nights.

The next morning Mom and Dad took me back to my room at Mrs. Welch's. She accepted our gift of one of the salmon and agreed to show me how to bake it for our dinner that night. I said a sad "Goodbye" to my family and sent them on their way back home without me. I really wasn't upset about it. Instead, I was filled with a sense of adventure in an entirely new kind of country with my teaching as my security.

Several days later I received a postcard from Mom saying that the fish made the trip in fine shape. They had bought ice and repacked it each night. As soon as they got home they called all of the family together, and they had a big fish fry, enjoyed by all, especially Grandpa, but "you would never want to smell that army blanket!"

Chapter Twenty-six

Getting Acquainted

My first meal with Mary Welch was highlighted by that fresh jack salmon. The captain of our boat told us that a jack salmon was a yearling, rather like a teen-ager. It had not yet gone back upstream in fresh water to fertilize or lay eggs in the same gravel bed where it had hatched. It was pink instead of red, and perhaps not quite as flavorful as a mature fish, but I didn't care. A salmon was a salmon and this was one that <u>we</u> caught. I definitely was not a connoisseur, as Mary probably was, but she didn't dash my enthusiasm for the fish. As she began to fix it for baking, she said,

"It's great that your dad and the captain did such a nice job cleaning this fish."

"I don't remember who caught this one, but my grandpa brought us up on 'He who catches, cleans!' He's the one who taught us how to bone a pan fish on our plates."

"Well, first we need a nice clean brown paper sack with no printing on it."

"Why does that make a difference if we're just going to use it to flour the fish?"

We're not gong to flour and fry it. We're going to bake it."

Mary pulled out the breadboard and handed me a butcher knife and two lemons.

"You can cut these in half lengthwise and then cut each half into very thin slices. I'll do the same with an onion as soon as I peel it."

When that was done, she made deep slashes about a half inch apart all down both sides of the fish. She invited me to help her stuff alternating half slices of onion and lemon into the gashes with the straight edges going in first. This meant that we could get all of the flavors into the fish with the outer edge of the slices flush with the curve of the fish's sides.

I hated to correct her but I said, "Don't we have to scale it first?"

"No, the scales will be nice and tender. Salmon scales are very tiny. We Scandinavians usually cook it, head and all. "

I knew she was teasing when she laughed at the squeamish look that I wasn't able to hide.

"I thought you'd feel that way, so I cut the head off before we started dressing it. No, we don't eat the scales and we don't have to scale the fish either, at least in the usual way."

"That's a big relief! I thought I was just going to have to pretend that fish scales were very tasty and they don't scratch your throat as they are going down. I do want to be courteous," I said with a shy chuckle.

"No, here we go. We wrap it up in brown paper like this, tie a whole bunch of string around it so the paper is nice and tight, and then we pop it into the oven. When it is done we'll cut all the string and peel the paper off. The scales and skin will be stuck to the paper, and we'll have a nice bare fish just waiting for us to cut into it."

"Oh, boy. How clever! Just like that!"

The dinner was great and the salmon was delicious.

The first day of school was chaotic, as it usually is. I didn't have any sense of impending trouble except for adjusting to teaching third grade. The children seemed to be much younger than I expected and definitely were not as independent as my former fourth graders had been. I couldn't believe that they could grow up so much in just one year.

The weather was bright and sunny, except for the heavy fog in the mornings. My days stretched ahead, full of exploring the exciting Northwest. I had my teaching for emotional and financial security. I wasn't at all homesick because I had left a big, black burden back there in the Midwest, and my heart was light.

Then reality caught up with me. Late in the afternoon during the second week of school one of my mothers stopped in to see me. I was tired and up to my neck trying to make workable lesson plans for my new class. There was a vast difference between fourth graders and third graders and I was struggling with the immaturity and lack of independence of my students. After visiting for a few minutes the mother stated the purpose of her visit.

"Miss Conway, we are looking for someone to be the leader of our girls' Brownie troop? It's obvious that you love children or you wouldn't be in teaching."

Is this what I think it is?!!!

"The other mothers sent me to invite you to help us out with this."

I'll pretend I don't know what she is driving at!

"You need someone as a leader? But I'm new to the community. I don't know anyone to recommend for a job like that."

How can I get out of this gracefully and not make any of my mothers angry before I've even met them?

"Well, what we really would like is for you to be the Brownie leader for our little girls."

ME? I have more little girls clamoring for my attention than I can handle as it is. But I can't admit that to them! That sounds like one more set of lesson plans to worry about! Is this traditional in this school or in this community…for teachers to be youth leaders also?

"Did Mr. Shipley suggest you talk to me?"

"No, but his wife, one of our first grade teachers, has been a Brownie leader for a long time. She says she enjoyed leading our Brownies for a change of pace from her first graders."

So she's getting out of the job and pushing it off on the new kid on the block?

"I'm sorry, Mrs. Johnson. I'd love to help out…

I'm lying through my teeth!

"and I'm very honored that you would choose me…

Actually, I'm really mad that you would put me in this position.

"but I'm really too busy to take this on at the present time."

"But Miss Conway, it's only a few hours after school once a week. And you could hold your meetings and plan events with them right here in your classroom every Wednesday."

What are you mothers doing with your spare time? Playing bridge all afternoon?

"You'd have fun with them. It would be more like having parties with them rather than acting as their teacher."

Giggling, squealing little girls! Having fun because teacher is playing with them instead of maintaining discipline?

"I'm sorry, Mrs. Johnson, but one look at my desk should tell you that this is the worst possible time for me to try to be responsible for another group of girls after teaching all day. I need this time to grade papers, make lesson plans and wind down a bit before I head for home for the evening."

"Oh, our girls will be so disappointed."

"I'm sorry about that too, but you might check with Mr. Shipley for another recommendation if you can't find a mother to take it on.

"Well, thanks anyway!"

As Mrs. Johnson headed for the door, I replied, "See you at the PTA meeting next week!"

I knew I would probably be roasted at the coffee klatches and telephone gab fests for a week or two, but so be it. I was proud that I had stuck to my guns and said "No". Maybe I was learning!

Chapter Twenty-seven

The Cake

Mary Welch, my landlady, did the shopping and most of the cooking for our evening meals. I helped her finish up our dinners and cleaned up the kitchen afterwards. We visited and began to build a friendly relationship. I even told her about the problems I had between my parents and Floyd and how relieved I was to be out from under his influence at last.

She tried to help me get acquainted in Aberdeen. She invited me to go to church with her on Sunday but she kinda snorted when I told her that Floyd introduced me to the Unitarian Church and that we were members of it back home.

"That's no kind of church. They're not even Christians in that church."

I didn't know what her definition was of "Christians", but I sure wasn't about to get into a debate with her about it. I dutifully went with her to the Methodist Church, as the respectable new teacher in town should do. She took me to the fall potluck dinner and introduced me to all of her friends. I baked one of my favorite cakes and put it on a lovely crystal cake plate that she let me borrow. I took it as my contribution to the meal.

When it came time for desserts, the plates of goodies were passed around so that everyone could help themselves without having to get up from the tables. When the dinner was over, I couldn't find her cake plate anywhere! I tried to trace my cake from one table to another. I asked over and over,

"Did you have some of a shaved chocolate cake at this table?"

The usual response was, "Yes and it was so good. Did you make it?"

"Yes, I did, and thank you very much. But now I'm looking for Mary Welch's crystal cake plate. Where did you send it when it left here?"

I went to several more tables but the answer changed to, "No, we didn't get any of that one here. "

No luck! My trail had turned cold! I was worried. When I finally went out to the kitchen to see if any of the dishwashers had seen it, the two guys who manned the big coffee urns grinned sheepishly. One of them reached behind the urns and said, "Is this it?"

"Oh, yes! Thanks so very much for keeping my plate for me."

"That's OK, Ma'am. But we weren't interested in your plate. Everyone said your cake was so good. We were saving this chunk of cake for ourselves when we get this job done."

They scraped the remaining one fourth of my cake onto another plate and handed Mary Welch's sticky treasure to me. I was relieved, and flattered at the same time.

Shaved Chocolate Chiffon Cake

Allow 1 hour preparation and mixing time, 1 hour for baking, and 1 hour for cooling!

1 c. egg whites (7 or more) ½ t. cream of tartar	Separate the eggs, putting the whites and cream of tartar in the largest bowl for your mixer and the yolks in a small bowl or cup. The bowl for the whites must be absolutely clean. Even a trace of oil will prevent egg whites from whipping. Let the eggs come to room temperature while you measure everything else.
Set oven at 325'	Oil an angel food cake tin
2 oz. bitter baking chocolate	Grate onto a piece of waxed paper
1 oz. bitter baking chocolate	Reserve for the icing
<u>Wet Ingredients:</u>	<u>Dry Ingredients</u>
5 egg yolks	Sift flour before measuring. Pile it lightly the measuring cup..
½ c oil	2 ¼ flour (cake flour is best)
¾ c. cold water	1 ¾ c sugar
2 t. vanilla	3 t. baking powder
	½ t. salt
	Sift together three times on sheets of waxed paper.

Beaters must be clean and free of oil. Beat the egg whites until very dry and won't slide out of the bowl if it is tipped over. Transfer into another clean, dry bowl. Set aside.

Using the original egg white bowl, beat egg yolk mixture (wet ingredients) until light colored and fluffy. Gently add dry ingredients, beating slowly until just blended.

By hand, using a whisk, fold yolk mixture into beaten egg whites being careful to stir them as little as possible. At the last minute, fold in the shaved chocolate, stirring as little as possible. Let pouring into the pan complete the blending of the chocolate.

Bake at 325' for 55 minutes and then finish it off with 10 more minutes at 350'. Let hang upside down for at least 1 hour. Remove from pan. Cover with a thin coat of icing made of 1 oz. melted chocolate, ½ c. melted butter, 2 t. vanilla, ½ box powdered sugar and enough hot coffee (by the teaspoonful) to make a thin, runny frosting.

PART FOUR

Impaled
On the Horns
of the Devil

But He turned and said to Peter,
"Get behind Me, Satan.
You are a stumbling block to Me;
for you are not setting your mind
on God's interests;
but on man's".

Matt.16: 23. ---NAS

Chapter Twenty-eight

Surprise, Surprise, Surprise!

September, 1952

Shortly after school started, I walked home one evening, my bag stuffed with homework, as usual. As I approached Mary's house, I stopped and gasped! That huge black cloud that I left in Indiana came roaring at me like a tornado, darkening my sky over Aberdeen, Washington! It threatened to touch down and tear apart my new world of peace and calm. When I saw an all too familiar dark blue Buick with Indiana license plates parked in Mary's driveway, I knew that there, in our living room, waiting for me to come home, was Floyd Dubois!

What can I do? How did he find me? I felt safe from him because we had half the continent between us. What should I say? How should I act? I sure didn't count on this!

Using the back door, avoiding the living room as long as possible, I dropped my school work on the kitchen table and just stood there. I needed time to regain my composure. I smoothed down my hair, took a deep breath and tried to relax. Then I faced up to what had to be done and walked into the front room.

Floyd was sitting in the lounge chair and Mary on the couch. I headed toward the couch and I wanted to say, "What the hell are you doing out here?" But I was a good girl and I didn't swear. I was trying to play it cool rather than let him know how I really felt.

"Well, fancy meeting you out here!"

"Hello, Bonnie! How are you doing?"

"So, I'm Bonnie again, am I?"

I started to sit down beside my landlady, more for a sense of protection or support than for anything else. But Floyd was already on his feet.

"Surprise, my Irish lassie!"

"You're telling m…."

He grabbed me and gave me a big hug and a kiss. Not getting much of a response from me, he released me to plop down beside Mary. He returned to his chair.

It looked like my landlady had been the courteous hostess, visiting with him while waiting for me to come home. I wondered what she thought when he introduced himself. She knew all about him because I confided in her in some of our evening conversations.

Did she hesitate to let him come in? Well, he's here now. I'll bet she's dying to see how this is going to turn out... So am I! Better think of something to say.

"Well, Floyd, what are you doing out here?"

That sounds non-committal enough.

"I'm taking classes at the University of Washington in Seattle. I've signed up for a course called 'The Bible as Literature'… and a few others."

"You're going to study the Bible! Since when?"

"No, not that way. I expect this to be a secular study of the Bible. None of that religious stuff. I'm anxious to see if I can get the prof to discuss all of the flaws and inconsistencies in the so-called 'Holy Book."

Boy, I'll bet Mary's hair is curling at that!

"Ah, if you two will excuse me, I think I'll go prepare dinner."

I was right. That was too much for her.

'Mary, don't fix anything for Bonnie and me."

As if he had been invited to join us!

"I'm taking Bonnie out on the town tonight to celebrate our reunion."

Chapter Twenty-nine

Manipulation

Floyd led me to his car and held the door open for me. He was being so gallant! I crunched up into the corner by the window with my arms folded across my chest. I was silent all the way downtown, lost in a fog of confusion. I spoke to him only for giving him directions to the café on Main Street, down near the lumber mills. Being new to the area, it was the only place I knew of in this small lumber and fishing town.

Floyd led me to a booth in a far back corner of the room. I was still upset and didn't feel like talking to him. I plopped down at the table and made no effort to be cordial.

Why am I giving him any time at all? Why hadn't I kicked him out as soon as I saw him? Why am I always so polite and concerned about other's feelings? Did I feel obligated because he had come all of the way out here just to be with me? I guess that's the answer.

He sat across the table from me. He smiled at me but I tried to avoid looking at him. His eyes seemed menacing, somehow. They didn't match his smile or his tender actions toward me. He leaned across the table, locking his eyes on mine, saying something that didn't even register in my mind. Mentally, I was numb to everything going on around me. Physically, I shivered and felt invaded somehow. I looked down and pulled my eyes away from his.

I am able to resist his gaze after all, aren't I?

I looked down and mumbled, "I'm not really hungry, Floyd," as though I thought food was all that he had on his mind.

As a distraction, I attempted to study my menu. I finally gave up trying to concentrate on it.

"I can't make up my mind. Go ahead and order for me."

While we were waiting he reached across the table, took my hand and said,

"Bonnie, you have no idea how much I've missed you. Even last summer when your parents wouldn't let you date me. You really broke my heart."

I slumped in my seat. I tried to protest. "But Floyd"

"No, I mean it. I couldn't believe that you would let them dominate you so much that you would try to kill my love for you. For weeks I couldn't sleep because I thought I had lost you. You're my Irish lassie forever, you know!"

Forever? Never! That phrase "forever" shook me out of the stupor I was in. I jerked my head up and withdrew my hand.

"How did you find me out here?"

"It was easy. I told your principal back home that I was a friend of yours and asked her if she had heard from you. She told me that you had taken a job teaching in Aberdeen, Washington. So I called the district office here and said I wanted your address so I could write to you. They gave it to me."

"But they had no business…"

"You can't blame them. They didn't know you were running away from me…"

Oh, boy! I can't let him think that he's that important to me!

"No, let's get this straight, Floyd Dubois," I exclaimed. "I was not running away from you!

Liar, liar, pants on fire! (a childhood chant, not related to my present condition!)

"That's not why I moved out here. This is just a good way to really get to know another part of the country. And, I was trying to leave behind me all of the trouble and heartache that *you* caused between my parents and me. I love them very much. You almost gave my dad a heart attack!"

"I know, Bonnie, and I'm sorry that they didn't like me… But that's all behind us now. We can start over again with a clean slate, no opposition from anyone. Just the two of us…"

"But I don't want…"

"We'll have such fun exploring the Northwest together. We have so much in common; our love for travel, our dedication to higher education, our desires to help mankind, you as a teacher and me as a psychologist and counselor."

That sound just like him, spreading it on thick…

When our dinners arrived, I tried to use eating as a way to avoid eye contact. But, with his eyes boring in to mine, it wasn't long before my thinking began to change.

It's not every girl who has a man follow her half way across the country because he wants to make amends. I wouldn't have to sneak around to be with him. We could enjoy Seattle together. I could invite him to go with Clarence and me into the Olympic forest. I guess we could have fun together.

After dinner we drove around Aberdeen, exploring what there was of it. Floyd found a secluded spot where we could look at the beautiful bay in the moonlight and "talk". When he tried to kiss me, I pushed him away.

"Oh, come on Bonnie. Just a little kiss for an old friend from long ago?"

It wasn't all that long ago, but I complied with "just a little" kiss. In spite of myself, I began responding to several more kisses and he pulled me toward him to hold me tight. I leaned into his shoulder. I noticed that old warm feeling of arousal was spreading upward from my heart. Trying to remain outwardly cool and impersonal in spite of it, I remarked, "It is cozy here looking out over the bay, isn't it?"

Without attracting my attention, he reached down beside his seat, and pulled a lever. We both jolted as the whole front seat lurched backward, giving us more leg room!

Oh, no! I know what that means! He's going to get serious!

I broke up his romantic endeavors by pushing him away and saying that I had to teach in the morning and that he had better take me home.

He sighed in resignation, started the car and headed for Mary's.

We kissed goodnight several times after he parked in Mary's driveway. I felt safer there. When he began rubbing my back as he kissed me, I reluctantly said, "I had better say goodnight, Floyd." I slipped out of the car and headed toward the house.

Floyd followed me and before I could open the front door, he grabbed one of my arms, spun me around, and held me tight as he gave me a hard, forceful kiss. I broke loose, opened the door, and said, "I'll be seeing ya!" I left him standing there, empty handed.

"Oh, hello, Mary. You're still up?"

Mary was knitting and listening to the radio. I was embarrassed at my hot, flushed cheeks. She knew we had been necking, even after all the terrible things I had told her about Floyd.

"Yes, I was waiting up for you. I was worried about you."

"Well, thanks…, but you don't have to worry any more. Ah, we had a fine dinner… and then I showed him around town a bit… But… I'm tired and I'm going right to bed. I have to get up early in the morning."

"All right… Have a good sleep. I'll see you in the morning."

So, she was worried about me. Does that mean I have to continue to confide in her? She's only my landlady, not my mom! If I date Floyd, it's none of her business.

From that point on, my easy friendship with Mary was over. I felt guilty. I expected her to object to Floyd, just as my parents had. Any hope she had of real companionship with me faded in my newly restored desire to see as much of Floyd Dubois as possible, whether she approved or not!

Chapter Thirty

Pike Place Market

Fall, 1952

In the fall I was especially eager for my weekends to roll around because that was the only chance Floyd and I had to see each other. He came down to Aberdeen every Saturday unless I managed to get up to Seattle to see him. It was like dating back in Indiana. Once again he courted me and was a very understanding and persistent suitor. I was charmed by his visits and his attention. It didn't take long for him to reestablish in me those old feelings of romance. Soon he convinced me that he sincerely loved me and desperately needed me at his side forever. I felt like a lump of "Silly Putty" in his hands, because I was thrilled with being so treasured.

In late October I found a perfect way to get to Seattle to be with Floyd. I met a young teacher who drove up the east side of the Olympic Peninsula to Bremerton every weekend. Betty, the driver, couldn't wait to see her husband, a sailor, whose ship was berthed there. On Friday, we left together just as soon as school was out. She floored the gas pedal and ignored all speed limits as soon as she was out of town. I held my breath and prayed a bit, until I remembered that our road would be going through an uninhabited national park.

That seemed less risky for speeding. She was glad to accept gas money from me in exchange for the ride up north and back. From Bremerton I rode the ferry to Seattle.

Very late one Friday night Floyd met me at the terminal. We spent the weekend enjoying each other, playing house, and exploring Seattle together. At his insistence, I was able to spend several weekends with him in his apartment in the Green Lake area. He encouraged me to consider transferring to the Seattle school district between semesters, and moving in with him. But of course, I insisted that we would have to get married. Because of my moral upbringing, I was ashamed of our pretend marriage on weekends, but he seemed rather proud of it.

I was filled with awe on the Friday evening trips up the Olympic Peninsula to Bremerton. Betty roared up the two lane black top road as we wound northward between the deep green shade of the Olympic forest on our left, and the sparkling blue waters of Puget Sound on our right. We rolled down our car windows so we could soak up the musky, piney fragrances of the Olympic rainforest or the bracing fresh breezes from the salt water of the Sound, whichever was closest.

Several times we passed well built side roads, but they were posted. Lumber companies' signs blocked their entrances.

Betty nodded to one as we flew past it.

"You know, Barbara, I've always wondered what's down those roads, but they have locked chains across them."

She shook her head and sighed.

"Me too, but I have a cousin out here who promised to take me and a friend on a lumber road like that deep into the forest."

Frowning and puzzled, she said,

"How does he think he can get away with it?"

"He's a real live lumberjack. He works for Weyerhaeuser Lumber Company, and I guess he has a key, or something."

"Really? That's great!"

"He said he wants to show me the unspoiled wilderness and to tell me the lumber company's version of cutting timber in the national forests."

"Gee, you're lucky! That should be an interesting contrast to what we read in the newspapers."

"Yes, all we ever get from them is propaganda from the conservationists and politicians. I can't wait. I think I'll ask Floyd if he would like to go along."

Because I had some time to kill before catching the ferry, Betty let me out where she crossed the main street of downtown Bremerton. I walked several blocks to the ferry terminal, window shopping along the way. I almost passed a "greasy spoon" type of café, or maybe it was a tavern. It was typical of what you might see in any navy town. But I stopped and did a double take. I couldn't believe it. There, in the dusty window was a messy, hand-lettered sign advertising pizza! I didn't realize they even knew what pizza was on the West Coast! I hadn't had any since I left home and I was tempted. But I didn't like the looks of the place. I summoned some will power and continued on, but I didn't forget about that sign.

Floyd greeted me with a great big hug and kiss right there in public! I was embarrassed. I was excited about getting to the privacy of his apartment. As I cuddled down beside him on our way "home", I gazed at Seattle's sparkling hills at night.

"Seattle is my own personal utopia. Isn't it beautiful?"

Floyd patted my knee and answered with a sly tone,

"Yes, and a very romantic one, too!"

Modestly, I tried to ignore what he was implying, but I didn't move his hand. Instead, I said,

"Aren't we lucky to be out here instead of back home?"

"Yes, but the best part is that we're together with no one to interfere."

"I'm so glad we can enjoy it together. That makes it doubly special."

On Saturdays we ambled hand-in-hand along the waterfront. We huddled over simmering bowls of thick, creamy clam chowder at "Ivar's", the famous seafood restaurant that had been there since pioneer days. On our way up the steep incline formerly called "skid row", we imagined the logs being skidded down to the bay in Seattle's lumbering days. We speculated about how the expression "being on skid row" originated.

After a long climb up from the bay, we came to a very busy street on the edge of a bustling downtown shopping district. Our new destination was the famous Pike Place Market. We were fascinated by fresh fish and beautiful produce for sale in the open air shops and booths. We joined the other spectators on the sidewalk in front of a big seafood and butcher shop. It was apparent from the excited chatter that something special was about to happen. We waited for someone to buy a large fresh salmon. The butcher reached into the case and pointed to each fish nestled in crushed ice. When the customer indicated which one she wanted, we all craned our necks to see what would happen next.

The butcher weighed the fish, got the customer's approval, and her cash, and then held the slippery thing over his head. He swerved it around to make it look like it was swimming. It was as though he was showing us that it was very, very fresh. Suddenly the fish appeared to leap out of his hands, and sail about 20 feet across the showcases to the other side of the shop. There a second butcher caught it and "wrestled" it down onto a pile of butcher paper. In a flash he controlled his "catch", wrapped it in paper with all of the ends tucked in and handed it to the customer with a flourish. All of us laughed, applauded them for their little show and went on our way, chuckling and looking for more amusement.

There were different levels of shops below the market that were stair-stepped down the sharp slope to the bay. We found a lot of souvenir and craft shops filled with curios from all over the world. Some sold beautiful shells and corals from tropical seas. For the tourists they even offered household trinkets made from shells; like ashtrays, picture frames and whimsical little animals. In the antique shops we saw all kinds of old marine souvenirs like antique anchors, whale oil lanterns and rusty couplings. We were fascinated with collection boards where sailors (?) displayed all kinds of knots, supposedly used on ancient sailing ships. It seemed to be a place where, in times gone by, sailors came to trade their rope hammocks, nets, and handcrafts for whatever sailors long for during their long months at sea. Of course there were many dark, dingy taverns where modern sailors, and tourists, could wet their whistles and maybe forget, temporarily, about whatever was haunting them. We almost expected to find an opium den hidden in the depths of the old buildings!

We spent Sunday mornings strolling alongside some of Seattle's sparkling lakes. The lush greenery and flowers in the parks in late fall were amazing to us. We compared them with the cold, barren parks of northern Indiana in the late fall.

As the idyllic weekends wound down, Floyd always sent me back on the ferry by 4:00 PM. It never occurred to me to question what he did after I left. I didn't suspect that he had another social life every Sunday afternoon and evening that couldn't include me. Monogamy wasn't his style, as I was to learn later!

Chapter Thirty-one

Pizza?

On Sunday evening, on my way back to Bremerton on the ferry, I was excited to see if I would get to see Mount Rainier on this trip. "Her Majesty," a skier's paradise, was usually shrouded in the fall or winter with heavy draperies of fog, or rain, or low cloud cover. That time, looking toward the southeast, I saw her sparkling snow covered peak. I was thrilled, flatlander that I was.

On the way back to Aberdeen, I told Betty about how wonderful it was to get to see Mount Rainier.

"It really topped off the ferry ride. That's always fabulous, in its own right!"

"Yes, really relaxing. Several times, when Bill, my husband had Saturday off, we took the ferry over to Seattle and back, just for the fun of it."

"Betty, have you ever tried the clam chowder that they sell on the ferry?"

"No, we haven't. Is there something special about it?"

"It's delicious! I read a story about it once that made me curious."

"What was the story about?"

"Well, it seems that the chowder was very famous, even across the country. A famous chef heard about it and when he visited Seattle, he decided to check it out. He wasn't at all disappointed. It was truly unique."

"In what way?"

"That's what he couldn't figure out. It wasn't the abundance of fresh chopped clams and it wasn't the rich creaminess. It had bits of bacon in it but that wasn't anything new. He wanted recipe, so he asked for a copy of it."

"He had to find out what was in it?"

"Yes, but the chef who was responsible refused to give it to him. He wouldn't give up his secret. So the famous chef offered to buy it. No luck. He kept upping the ante thinking that if he paid enough he'd be able to get it."

"And did he?"

"Yes, for an undisclosed sum. Now, this was years ago when a dollar went a lot farther than it does today. They say that when he finally had the envelope in his hand, he tore it open, scanned prized recipe rapidly, and said,

"Oh, Damn! I paid a thousand dollars for a little pinch of nutmeg!"

We both laughed at the tale and Betty said she and Bill would have to make another ferry boat ride to Seattle as soon as possible.

Then I told her about the pizza sign that I had seen.

"What do you mean, 'pizza'?"

"Well, it's a big round meat, tomato sauce and cheese, pie-like thing; only the crust really is a thin yeast bread crust, rather than a pastry. Back home our favorite was covered with a special tomato pizza sauce, spicy Italian sausage, sliced green peppers, mushrooms and mozzarella cheese. Italians enjoyed it in their homes for years, but Gary was where it was first made and sold commercially."

"I've never heard of it. It sounds great!"

"It is! In about 1945 an Italian owned 'The Flamingo', a tavern downtown. He installed special custom built ovens and began to serve pizza in his dining room behind the bar room. Because we were under age, we teenagers couldn't go near the bar. We had to use the family entrance off the alley!

"Pizza became the latest rage. The sausage was so spicy-hot that we had to order cokes to cool our tongues. Most adults probably boosted the owner's sale of beer significantly because of its spiciness. But no one else could cash in on his success. Some tried. Their first problem was finding another company that would dare to build the special ovens. The Mafia financed the Flamingo's owner originally and had a vested interest in his success. Several times other places tried to cut in on him, but their taverns burned to the ground in some very suspicious fires. One even got bombed out. But no one was ever prosecuted. Not in Gary."

"Wow! The Mafia! Operating not only in New York City, but in Gary, Indiana, too?"

"Yep, that's my hometown! Anyway, I'm so hungry for some good pizza. The next time, I'm going to get some even if that place looked pretty crummy."

"Well, good luck! Hope you don't get food poisoning!

Was that a prophecy? I hope not!

On Friday evening of my third weekend in Seattle with Floyd, I headed toward the Bremerton ferry terminal but I was dreaming of pizza. I stood outside the tavern trying to get up enough nerve to walk in.

It would be piping hot. The ovens would kill any germs that might be in it, wouldn't they?

Finally, I took a deep breath and opened the door. I chose a dark booth where I hoped no one would notice me. The bartender said that she only had cheese pizza, so I said I'd like one slice of it and a coke. I waited with my mouth watering in anticipation.

When it finally came, I couldn't believe my eyes! There, staring up at me, instead of a hot, chewy pizza crust, was a plain slice of white bread. Someone had smeared some spaghetti sauce on it, topped it with a slab of *American* cheese, and broiled in an oven! Not even some oregano sprinkled on top! I was *so* disappointed! That was the last pizza I even wanted to order anyplace, until I got home to good old Gary, Indiana! And I couldn't wait to tell Floyd about it! I knew he'd get a big kick out of it, too.

Sunday evening Betty and I shared our stories of our weekend adventures as we headed back to Aberdeen. We arrived late at night. We hoped we'd be able to wake up on Monday morning early enough to get to school on time!

Chapter Thirty-two

Prelude to a Wedding

OCTOBER, 1952

By late October I was becoming increasingly disturbed about Floyd's and my relationship. I was torn by my emotional need to be desired and loved, my moral façade of purity, and my own sexual passion. I couldn't see a solution, but Floyd figured it all out. He proposed that I simply tell Aberdeen that we were getting married, that I was leaving Aberdeen at the end of the first semester, and would get another teaching job in Seattle.

"That will give them their two week notice, won't it?"

I gasped! This wasn't like a retail or office job!

His dad is a 'contractor' and Floyd worked for him! Would his dad break a construction contract so easily?

"No, Floyd, it doesn't work like that. I signed a contract to teach the full year, and I can't break it."

"Contract, hell! That's just a piece of paper. It doesn't mean a thing!"

I sat up straighter. I guess my eyes flashed in anger.

"Oh, yes, it does! If I did that, it would ruin my reputation as a teacher and no one would ever hire me again. Besides, it just isn't ethical."

"Discussions" like this continued for several weeks during visits and numerous phone calls. Finally, I agreed to find out if Aberdeen would release me from my contract so that I could get married and move to Seattle.

To my surprise, empathy trumped over legality and the shortage of teachers. The superintendent in Aberdeen said they would release me to apply for a job in Seattle, if they could find a replacement for me.

I took a chance and interviewed for a position in Seattle. It was no problem at all. They tentatively hired me for a sixth grade position in West Seattle, pending my release from my contract with Aberdeen. The school was across downtown and Elliot Bay from where I would be living with Floyd in his apartment. But the bus service was good and I could handle that.

Thanks goodness I got an upper grade class. It will be good to get back where I belong. Those third graders have been driving me nuts with their immaturities.

Everything seemed to be working out, so I told Floyd he could make arrangements for us to get married. He told me that it would be a civil union with absolutely no religious connotations of any kind. I wasn't surprised. I couldn't expect otherwise from Floyd Dubois. It seemed like more of a business deal than a wedding. I wasn't excited or radiant or anything like that. I had stood my ground and wouldn't be just shacking up with him, and besides, he had been begging me to marry him for a long time. Because I thought we had so much in common like a thirst for higher education and learning, mutual respect for each other (*was I blind?*), a commitment to serve mankind and a desire for extensive traveling, I just knew this marriage would last. I still believed that I had found a man who understood me, and loved me (*and needed me!*).

We never discussed our finances because that seemed too personal when we were single. After his schooling was done, I assumed then we would talk about saving up to build or buy a house someplace or other. I never told Floyd that I wanted to teach for awhile and to start of family with up to four children. I was afraid that he would consider children a burden that would cramp his freedom. On that subject the discussion could come later.

On Saturday morning Floyd said he had a surprise planned for me.

"Bonnie, let's go downtown this afternoon and buy our wedding rings!"

"Oh, Floyd, that will be so much fun! You're going to let me help you pick them out?"

"Of course! The woman should have as much to say about it as the man! Besides, we're partners in this, aren't we?"

"We sure are! I love the way you expect us to be equals in our marriage."

I was on cloud 8 ½! We walked from the parking garage to one of the largest jewelers in Seattle, holding hands all the way.

"I should tell you right off that I don't like diamonds."

I should have known it! He's trying to save money and to let me down easy.

"You don't? Why?"

"Because they don't have any color and they're too common. Every bride gets a diamond for an engagement ring and more of the same in her wedding band."

Well, I guess I've already had my diamonds and they didn't seem to have any magical properties that ensured a lasting marriage!

"Well, what do you have in mind then?"

"First off, they must be matching bands, but not just plain gold bands, something unusual and unique."

Boy, this is going to be interesting! We've never had any discussions about finances, either his or mine. I have no idea if he has any savings at all. I just know that his dad sends him a check every month and that he seems to be pretty thrifty on our entertainment and dinners out. Of course, he insists that we go dutch, which I expect, because I'm the one who has a job. Hey! He'd better not expect us to go dutch on the rings, also!

"No, Bonnie, I guess we'll just have to wait and see what the jeweler suggests. Here we are!"

He offered me his arm and we sailed in as though we were regular clients.

Wow! This is an expensive place! Look at how elegant everything is!

While we were looking at rings in the showcase, a salesman in a somber black suit (but not a tux!) glided up to us on the other side of the display case. Floyd stated his restrictions as to our rings. We finally ordered custom-made, hand-designed matching rings of white gold with small emeralds embedded in raised vines and ivy leaves. The "carvings" and emeralds completely encircled the rings.

I had no idea what he had to pay for them, but I was thrilled. I thought that Floyd's was perhaps too fancy for a man's ring and I questioned him on whether his was practical and how well he thought it would hold up.

"Oh, don't worry about it, Bonnie. I'll never do hard labor with my hands and I'll probably only wear it for dress, or when we're out and we want to advertise that we are married."

I was in such a fog that I didn't realize the full import of what he was saying until later.

In late October my superintendent found a replacement for me at A. J. West School in Aberdeen beginning in February, and so I was free to make the move to E.C. Hughes School in West Seattle when the second semester began.

Several days later during our school lunch period I was discussing a dilemma with Norma Lundeen, one of our kindergarten teachers. She was a tall, blond Swede and a former airline stewardess supervisor! I admired her sense of fashion and turned to her for advice.

"Norma, I want something new to wear for when Floyd and I get married, but I haven't saved enough money to buy anything. I can afford to buy some fabric and make it myself. I think I'll ask Mary if I can use her sewing machine."

"You can sew? What do you have in mind?"

"Well, certainly not anything all white and fluffy!"

"A cocktail length dress?"

"No, everything I've looked at for ideas seems too elegant or too fussy. I really don't want to look like a bride at all. What do you think about a suit?"

"Wow! Can you tackle something like that?"

"I think so. Mom taught me to tailor. I've been looking at fabrics. I'm thinking of a forest green wool coat and a matching suit in a lighter weight fabric. How about that?"

"It sounds great! You sure are taking on a big job. Good luck! If you need any help on fitting or marking the hems, you know Jackie and I will try to help you."

I bought the fabric and began the major sewing project of my life.

Chapter Thirty-three

I Do, Again!

NOVEMBER, 1952

Our long awaited special weekend approached. I took Friday off but
I wanted to be in Seattle on Thursday night before getting married
on Friday. I felt like being extravagant so I took a commuter plane to
Seattle. No bus for me! As we took off from the airport, I could see the
Olympic Mountains and sparkling blue waters of the Pacific Ocean.
The plane turned northward, and the Cascades (coastal mountain
range) came into view. Settling down in contentment, I saw the light
from the setting sun leave the cities and villages, and watched dusk
invade the valleys.

I saw Olympia and Tacoma pass below. I heard an excited murmur
on my side of the plane. I gasped when I looked up toward the
eastern horizon. A spectacular sight greeted me. It looked like a giant's
strawberry sundae! Mount Rainier stood alone and its snow capped
peak shone with a rosy alpenglow. Low-lying, fluffy white clouds
surrounded the base of the mountain. They reminded me of scoops of
vanilla ice cream. The glaciers hugging the sides of the mountain were
like streaks of radiant strawberries and syrup sliding down from the

peak of the frozen concoction. All that was missing was the whipped cream and cherry to top it off!

My imagination really ran wild, but only for a few minutes. As I watched, the light on the clouds slowly dimmed. Then the rosy glow began to fade. Soon I was left with only a memory of a personal miracle and the black silhouette of a majestic mountain in the darkening sky.

The twinkling lights of Seattle awaited me as my magical trip came to a close. At the airport Floyd waited for me with open arms. I was exited and as radiant as my favorite mountain had been. We splurged on great seafood at Ivar's, and I entertained Floyd by trying to describe every minute of my wonderful flight into Seattle.

We slept in and took our time getting dressed on Friday morning. Floyd admired the coat and suit that I made as my bridal outfit for that evening. We had an appointment with a State Superior Court judge to marry us after hours on Friday. As soon as school was out, Norma, and Jackie and Bill Nolte planned to leave Aberdeen and barrel up to joins us.

They came to be our witnesses. We met them in the lobby of the courthouse and visited for a few minutes. In high spirits we laughed and joked in the elevator on the way up to the judge's chambers, but turned all somber and respectful as soon as we entered his outer office.

The judge greeted us with courtesy. The ceremony was short. Floyd was told he could kiss the bride, which he did but I had a rather empty feeling like, "That's all there is?"

Afterward, the five of us had a fine dinner in the Olympic Hotel dining room. Floyd would have only the best! On his dad's money!

I didn't tell Mrs. Welch that we intended to get married that weekend. I guess I considered her my surrogate mother figure. She had never been cordial to Floyd and I knew she wouldn't approve of me marrying an atheist. I pretended it was an elopement rather than a defiance. Because Floyd insisted that we keep it a secret from both of our families, and because I didn't want Mom and Dad to worry, I didn't tell them either, not until many long months later!

That night, after dinner and on our wedding night, I invited my friends to go up with us to see the room that Floyd had reserved for us. It wasn't a bridal suite but I didn't expect it to be anything special. They approved of it, and pulled out a deck of cards! They put a suitcase on the bed for a table. Sprawled all over <u>our</u> bed, they proceeded to play rummy and they invited us to join them. It looked like they had settled in for the night! This was our wedding reception?! It seemed to be a test of our courtesy. Were we supposed to laugh with them when they finally said goodnight? Well, I did and thought it was a funny joke, but Floyd let them know he didn't appreciate it one little one bit.

Our first night of husband and wife was a disaster. He was angry, rough, and demanding, as though he now owned me and my job was to pleasure him. My gentle suitor was no more! Instead I thought he was even a bit unorthodox and kinky!

The next morning wasn't any better. We were interrupted in our lovemaking by a knocking on our door about 9:00 A. M. and Floyd wouldn't answer it or let me get up. The phone rang and Floyd ignored it. Someone (a bellhop?) tried to rouse us three times and finally gave up. Each time I pleaded with Floyd to let me answer the knock or the phone. Each time I backed down because I didn't want anyone else to hear him roar at me in anger. When we opened the door much later, on our way to check out, a very cold, congealed, formerly elegant breakfast for two was sitting on the floor near our door. A large bunch of yellow chrysanthemums and a Hallmark wedding congratulations card from my friends accompanied our ruined meal.

Oh, no! They planned to spend the night at Jackie's parents' home here in Seattle! What if it hadn't been a bellhop? What if they went out early this morning and brought us some flowers and our breakfast as a peace offering?

I was horribly embarrassed. I hoped it had been a bellhop instead. I never admitted to Norma and Jackie that we heard the knocks on the door and that Floyd wouldn't let me answer the door. I hoped they had arranged it all, even the fresh flowers, as they left us on our wedding night and weren't actually standing out there knocking on our door. I didn't admit that we made no effort to eat that stone cold breakfast. But I did thank them for it, and the flowers and card, with real sincerity.

It started out being an unusual kind of marriage and it only got stranger as time wore on.

Chapter Thirty-four

Downtown Aberdeen

Early Sunday afternoon after our wedding weekend, Floyd took me back to Aberdeen and we told Mary that we had eloped. Then he hurried back to Seattle because he <u>said</u> he had to study that night.

During the following week I began to feel like the traditional bride. I floated around dreaming of the bliss that was to follow. I surprised everyone at school with news of our marriage and I made preparations to move from my rented room at Mary's to an apartment for the two months before I would be able to join my husband in Seattle. I rented a furnished apartment in a moderately tall building in downtown Aberdeen. The apartments were located over a large store on Main Street and were considered very comfortable and desirable.

On Friday evening I sponged out my sheer pink nightgown, dipped it in perfumed rinse water, and hung it up to dry. I was dreaming of a lovely, romantic weekend with my new husband despite the disaster of our previous wedding night. I wasn't disappointed.

Floyd arrived early Saturday morning. We transported my footlocker and luggage to his car but before we left I turned to Mary and said,

"Well, we're off, Mary. I really appreciate how well you put up with me. You made me feel so welcome."

"And I enjoyed getting acquainted with you."

"I'm afraid I wasn't all the company that you wanted and I hope I wasn't too much of a trial or disappointment to you."

"Oh, don't worry about it, Barbara. I enjoyed your company here at home and introducing you to my friends at church socials. Now you have a grand time together. I'll be praying that you two have a long and happy marriage…, together! Now, get going!"

"Goodbye, Mary. I'll be seeing you!"

Floyd and I moved all of my Washington possessions into my apartment. He went out to get us some hamburgers for lunch and read the paper while I unpacked. When everything was taken care of we went out for a drive and ended up at Gray's Harbor where I had camped with my family only a few months before. I deliberately put out of my mind the fact that Floyd wouldn't let me tell Mom and Dad that we were married. Besides I didn't want to admit it to them either and I didn't want to spoil the romantic euphoria we were enjoying. We wandered around the harbor looking at the boats and kicking up sand on the beach. We sat on a large rock on the shore, holding hands and gazing at the waves tumbling toward us. We talked about traveling we would do to exotic places. We embraced and kissed each other over and over as the gulls screeched overhead. How romantic!

This time I had a chance to inquire beforehand about a nice restaurant, and so we found it, nestled in a little cove, overlooking the Pacific Ocean. The white tablecloths and candlelight enhanced our mood perfectly and we ate wonderful seafood; Dungeness crab cocktails for appetizers, crisp green salads, and gently grilled fresh salmon fillets with baked potatoes and sour cream. The management gave the bridal couple, us! a huge slice of chocolate cake to share. We coasted out of there to the privacy in my apartment. We were mutually thrilled with sweet and tender love making and finally fell asleep, cuddled like spoons in a silver chest.

We slept in a bit on Sunday morning, had breakfast together in the corner café downtown, and then Floyd left for Seattle, early in the afternoon, as usual.

Early one stormy evening, after school, I caught the bus for downtown. I was prepared for the rain with my raincoat and bright yellow umbrella, but I was totally unprepared for what greeted me as we approached my bus stop. The bus sloshed through pounding rain and several blocks of foot deep water. It stopped for me to get off right in the middle of it all. I saw that I was going to have to go wading home so, on the steps I paused to slip off my new shoes so I wouldn't ruin them. I gingerly stepped off of the bus in my stocking feet, juggling my shoes, my school papers to be graded at home that night, my purse, and my umbrella. I had all I could do to hang onto everything, protect the papers from the driving rain, keep my balance in the raging stream even on the sidewalks, and struggle to keep my umbrella from turning inside out! Even then, I noticed that the fresh, clean scent of the bay seemed closer than ever.

All of the store entrances along Main Street were sandbagged. A geyser of water about two feet tall was feeding the flood. I scrambled over sandbags to get to the entrance of the lobby and elevator to my apartment. Now I knew why the lobby sat several steps above street level! I approached the clerk at the front desk, put my papers and shoes on his counter and folded my umbrella. I shed my raincoat, shook the water off of it and said,

"Wow! Hi! Bill. What's going on out there besides raining and blowing?"

"Oh, it's just the tide coming in!"

"What do you mean, 'the tide coming in'?"

"Well, downtown Aberdeen was built on sawdust fill from the saw mills. Sometimes after a big rain the ground used to shake when heavy trucks went down the street, but they're forbidden here now."

"Oh, really?" I teased.

"No, I'm not kidding. But what's worse, we're only a few feet above sea level here. When it's raining cats and dogs like this, the storm sewers fill up because there's not much of a drop to sea level. Add to that a high wind blowing down the bay from the west and an unusually high tide, and, well, we have little geysers all up and down the street. That's nice clean salt water and rain water that you see gushing up out of the storm sewers!"

"Golly, how often does that happen?"

"Oh, it's not often that you get all three factors acting at once. But it's often enough so that we're prepared. We can handle it, and it *is* kinda fun, isn't it?"

"Well, I guess so! It sure is different. But I had better get upstairs. I'm drenched to the bone."

"Good bye. Have a nice cozy evening. Hope you don't have to go out later!"

"No, I'd eat in if all I had available were cornflakes! See you tomorrow."

I went up on the elevator and turned up the heat in my apartment as soon as I walked through the door. I was shivering and the sparsely furnished place was dark and chilly.

As soon as I get warmed up I'll get myself something to eat. An empty apartment sure is a lonely place. Floyd is in Seattle and I am stuck in Aberdeen all by myself. I wish I could call Mom and Dad and talk to them. I miss Mary and our visits in the evening. She really put up with a lot from me. I wasn't a very sensitive companion for a lonely widow. Too much involved in my own life to try to understand what she was going through.

I made the coffee and turned on the radio to a station that I knew played music from the 40's.

That should help me calm down and get my mind off of myself. It didn't work.

Well, here I am in my own little place for the first time in my life. I can do anything I want, any time I want. Isn't it great to be independent and free?

But I'm married again. I guess that independent and free stuff is only during the weekdays. As soon as the first semester is over, I'll move to Seattle and start being a working housewife again.

As the coffee perked, I heated up a can of chicken noodle soup for my dinner. I continued to feel very sorry for myself. Eating alone wasn't much fun. I finished off my supper with some soda crackers and treated myself with some brie left over from my married weekend. I graded my third graders' papers. That done, I scrunched down into the overstuffed couch, still looking for some other way to get warmed up even though the thermometer said the apartment was now 78 degrees. I began to think about Floyd.

That was a nice weekend we just had together. He was loving and attentive, not at all like he was on our wedding night. It's so great to be honest and legitimate. Married, not having to sneak around and hide our passions.

I can survive these six or eight weeks by myself as long as we have our weekends together here in Aberdeen. I'll pretend to be happy in my independence. Then, in February I'll move in with my husband in Seattle and become a teacher-housewife again, as I am meant to be.

I tried to reassure myself of the bliss and secure peace that awaited us in Seattle, but I knew, over all, there was still a nebulous sense of distrust, an uneasiness when I wondered about Floyd's view of our future. I shuddered and sought the comfort of a warm bed. I collapsed, praying for a future of domestic tranquility.

Chapter Thirty-five

Christmas Agony

December, 1952

Floyd didn't tell his dad that he was married for fear that he would cut him off. He didn't want me to tell my parents because he was afraid that they would go to his dad and tell him about us. I didn't intend to tell my folks anyway because I knew they would be very upset and concerned for my safety. They knew that Floyd carried a gun.

My Christmas that year was a horrible one. The first semester wasn't over and I was still living alone during the week in my apartment in downtown Aberdeen. Floyd came down on weekends. His dad sent him one set of round trip air flight tickets so that he could go home for Christmas. Floyd left for Indiana, leaving me behind. Floyd insisted that we keep up the subterfuge with our parents.

I've never been so depressed in all my life. The weather is gray and gloomy. The fog is thick like milk gravy. It clings to everything and soaks the color out of anything that could be cheerful. The Christmas lights can't even cut through the gloop of the fog, or through my depression!

I felt totally isolated. I didn't have a car and couldn't get out of town. As a way of coping, I rented a sewing machine and made myself a Black Watch plaid jumper. But even that gave my mind time to simmer and stew over my problems.

How could Floyd do this to me? Well, if he is determined not to tell our folks, what else could he do? Say "No, thanks" to his dad for the round trip ticket? I guess not. So it's not his fault?

I asked God for an understanding attitude and a heart full of love and forgiveness for my husband. But then I brushed back my hair and finally sobbed when I heard Christmas carols assailing my ears from my only companion, the radio.

Oh, how I wish I could go home for Christmas, too. But I couldn't afford it. Most of my paycheck is going for this apartment. I haven't been able to save anything. Besides, how could I face Mom and Dad? I can't even call them because I feel so guilty. This whole vacation could have been so great. We'd go home together. I'd confess to Mom and Dad and they'd make the best of it. I just know they would. Instead, here I am, still lying to them. I feel like I'm sneaking around just like I did at home. That marriage license doesn't help a bit. It only makes everything worse, as far as they're concerned!

I made myself a cup of hot chocolate in an effort to lift my spirits. My thoughts turned to my former landlady.

I wonder if they tried to call me at Mary's. I didn't give her my new address when I moved out. I wonder what she would tell them. She knows we intend to keep our marriage a secret from everyone back home. If she tells them the truth, they'll be even more worried.

Jackie and Bill invited Norma and me to their apartment for dinner one night. They tried to include me in their pre-holiday festivities but I was so tied up in my own misery that I wasn't very good company.

They were sympathetic but I didn't want to spoil their Christmas spirit. Besides, they would soon be going home for Christmas, too.

Why am I letting Floyd put me in this position? It's as though he wants to isolate me and make me totally dependent on him alone. But there's one thing he can't take away from me! My teaching and my students! How I wish school was still on. That way I could occupy my mind with my kids instead of sitting here in my pink fuzzy bathrobe, feeling sorry for myself.

I can't even call Mary and visit with her. She's probably glad I moved. I was the one who killed that friendship because I knew she didn't approve of Floyd. I don't want to admit my misery to her.

Well, Christmas finally came and went. I didn't consider going to church because it wasn't essential and because I had no transportation. Several days later I reflected on advice Floyd had given me because he knew I was very upset about his leaving.

Floyd thinks he's such an expert psychologist. He told me that when I got upset or angry I was supposed to lie down in a bathtub full of cold running water, and stay there as long as I could stand it. He said that lowering my body temperature would enable me to control my emotions. Well, I even tried that and it didn't help one bit.

I tried to change my mood by eating out one night but my guilty conscience went along with me.

I can't imagine how upset Mom and Dad are at not hearing from me, even over the holidays! But I just can't call them, I just don't dare! How could I carry on a conversation with them and not let them know what I've done? I know I ruined their Christmas because getting all of the family around the Christmas tree has always been so important. This dinner in a fine restaurant doesn't compare with the meals that Mom and I put out together.

I was so mad at Floyd, for getting me in such a mess. I remembered that big fight back home. I realized this wasn't the first time Floyd got me into a big rhubarb with my folks. I felt like there was a smoldering peat bog fire in my brain.

I hate myself for letting him control me like this. I'm a real basket case. What would it be like to really crack up? Who would take care of me?

If he doesn't come back soon, it will be time to go back to school. I can hardly wait. At least there I'll be back in a safe and sane classroom with my kids. I sure miss them.

Floyd showed up about three weeks later. He expressed only contempt for my weakness when I tried to describe my agony while he was gone. He saw no reason for me not to have been content in Aberdeen all by myself, or to be angry-jealous while he flew back home for Christmas. Then he totally devastated me.

"Right after Christmas I wanted to take a little vacation so I went down to Florida for a couple of weeks."

"YOU DID WHAT? YOU WENT ON A *LITTLE* VACATION? WITHOUT ME? YOU LEFT ME HERE, AT CHRISTMAS TIME? ALL BY MYSELF? WHILE YOU WENT TO FLORIDA AND LET ME SIMMER IN MY LONELINESS?"

"Bonnie, it didn't occur to me that you would be so selfish and think only of yourself! If you really loved me, you wouldn't deny me a little fun, would you?"

"ME? SELFISH! And here I was dreaming of all of the traveling we were going to do together! We were going to see the world together, weren't we?"

"But Bonnie, something good came out of it, while you were just laying around here wallowing in self-pity!"

"And what might that be?"

Then I really came all apart. I was simply mute with disbelief when he told me that in Florida he met a "dance hall girl" and befriended her. He lived with her in her apartment for the 2 weeks he was there, and found out that she was very needy trying to raise her little girl by herself. He felt so sorry for her that he gave her all of his money as he left, and flew back to Seattle with empty pockets. He thought I should be proud at his efforts as a social worker and counselor.

"YOU MOVED IN WITH A PROSTITUTE?"

"Now, Bonnie, there you go again! Don't you have any compassion for people who are down and out?"

"DON'T TALK TO ME ABOUT 'COMPASSION'! WHAT ABOUT YOUR WIFE? DID YOU ALREADY FORGET THAT YOU'RE MARRIED?"

With arrogance he said he saw nothing wrong with sleeping with another woman and didn't know why I was so hurt. He said that what he really wanted was an open marriage anyway...

OH, God! This is the first I've heard about <u>*that!*</u>

He can't be serious!

God, how did I get into this mess?

Then, as I calmed down a little bit, my silent response was Polly Anna-like:

Thank you, God, for Floyd's return. I pray that he didn't bring a venereal disease home to me. I know I'll make this marriage work when we're living together as husband and wife in Seattle. Won't I?

I retreated into <u>MY</u> bedroom sobbing. I locked the door, threw myself into the middle of <u>MY</u> bed, and cried myself to sleep.

Chapter Thirty-six

Moving to Seattle

At last I could move into "our" apartment in Seattle. Between semesters Floyd picked me up, with my stuff, and he drove northward along the eastern shore of Puget Sound. We enjoyed the beauty of the wintertime greenery and the occasional glimpse of water to our left. But even then, I tried to not be worried about our relationship.

I'm sure things will get better between us when we're really living together. I already blew one marriage and I've defied absolutely everyone on this one. I just have to prove them wrong!

Wanting to get Floyd in a romantic mood and make this a loving adventure for both of us, I patted his thigh and cuddled up to his side.

"You know, Floyd, isn't it just great to be together like this and to really be moving to Seattle? It's like a dream come true."

"Yeh, I guess so," he said without any feeling.

Then, grinning at me suggestively and raising his eyebrows, he added, "I can hardly wait until we get back to my apartment!"

O.K., so I got a sexy response from my husband. Once upon a time I was so intrigued by him. He promised a life filled with love and understanding, and sexual excitement. But now what I really want is approval from him. Come to think of it, ever since I first met him, he has never given me unconditional approval. Even if I keep on trying I guess I'll never reach his standards of perfection as a companion, let alone as a wife! I try so hard to please him, even in sex. But even there he's always demanding things of me that I hate.

Every time that we visit with someone else, like in the garage while he's having his car serviced, I get a run-down later. Like, "Why did you say ..." or "You shouldn't have leaned against the fender like you did. It was like you wanted to be one of the guys instead of a woman," or "That was really insensitive when you... I just never measure up."

Underneath my efforts to create a romantic atmosphere, I felt trapped by anger like silent current that also ran counter to all of the excitement and joy that I tried to express to him. The truth was that I blamed Floyd for all of the guilt that I whipped myself with concerning my mom and dad. I couldn't face them, even in a phone call, without admitting my rebellion. I was digging my hole deeper and deeper. I didn't know how to explain why I transferred to Seattle in the middle of the school year, or the new address, or the new phone number. They had no way to contact me! I was numbed by the deceit and dishonesty of it all. I was very aware, I thought, of the heartache I was dumping on them. I didn't want to think about how agonized they were already, not hearing from me for three months! I just hoped they would think I had been terribly busy...but over Christmas? It was too horrible to think about. I decided to put it out of my mind and not let that mar my hope of building a happy marriage with Floyd in Seattle.

As usual, in an effort to divorce myself from my personal troubles at home, I deliberately shifted my focus to my classroom. I decided to talk about my new teaching assignment. At least there I was the expert and maybe I could stir up some support or encouragement.

I shifted in my seat to face Floyd instead of looking out the car window. I wanted him to know that I was demanding his serious attention.

"Floyd, did you know that I've never taught in the upper grades before?"

"No, but it won't be any different, will it?"

I frowned at him.

I thought he had a better feel for teaching than that!

"I don't know. I did my student teaching in fourth grade and taught two years of fourth grade at Glen Park School before moving out here.

"And so?"

"Well, in Aberdeen, I found out that I just couldn't handle third grade as well as I should. I was uncomfortable all semester."

"You mean you couldn't control those little kids?"

What a stupid response!

I shook my head with impatience.

"No, that wasn't it. Control wasn't the problem. They were such babies. Their attention span was so short. I had a hard time keeping them all busy enough so that I could meet with my reading groups. By comparison, my fourth graders seemed much more mature."

"And so now you are going to go into sixth grade. That's a jump!"

Oh, he understands the difference in ages after all.

I gazed at all of the trees rushing by as I composed what I wanted to say. I needed to tell him that I was confident in my teaching in the upper grades. I really craved any expression of respect from him. Respect about anything!

"That's the strange thing about it. When I first began teaching, I was scared of the bigger kids. Fourth graders seemed much safer and easier to handle. But here I am, not at all concerned. I'm amazed. I know I'll appreciate their independence in reading and written work and I'll have more time to work with small groups or individuals."

"Well, for your sake, I hope it works."

Nodding my head with assurance, I added,

"It will. I was warned in my interview that this would be a challenging class. In other words, they'll be a handful. _They_ think they ran out two teachers in the first semester, and they'll be waiting to take _me_ on, too."

"And you think _you_ can turn them around?"

I was challenged by the scorn I heard in his voice. But now he focused on the thickening traffic as we approached the city. I watched his profile to see if he was even listening to me. I proceeded anyway.

"I remember Mattie Hahnz, our junior high and high school auditorium and performing arts teacher. She could demand attention from a whole assembly of rambunctious high schoolers, even before a football rally! One thousand kids! All she had to do was stand very upright, tall, and silent before them and wait until they noticed that she wanted their attention. Her obvious waiting brought peer pressure on the noisy ones. Then she spoke in a little softer voice than usual to make them struggle to hear her. The acoustics in the auditorium were excellent. Whenever anyone caused the least disturbance, she came to a dead stop and made everyone wait again until she had 100% attention. It worked. Of course, she trained us in smaller groups ever since we came to junior high. Everyone loved her and respected her. We appreciated her professionalism. No one goofed off in _her_ auditorium. Nothing ruffled her."

"And you think that will work with a tough class of sixth graders?"

"I know it will, only instead of staring at them; I'll smile and let them know that we're friends, not challengers. I can hardly wait to try it out in the morning."

I awakened with excitement to my first day in a new school. I got up early before dawn and was on my way in the drizzle, walking to the bus stop by 6:30. I had about an hour bus ride before me with a transfer in downtown Seattle to West Seattle. I arrived at E.C. Hughes Elementary School and checked in at the office. The principal was cordial and took me to the second floor. He showed me my classroom and introduced me to Mrs.Morgan, who taught sixth grade next door and Sue Takahashi, who had a fifth grade classroom across the hall. After visiting for a bit I went back to my desk, opened up the lesson plans that I had prepared over the weekend, and waited for my "little cherubs" to push and shove each other into their classroom, on their turf!

Dear old Mattie Hahnz's magic worked and I knew we were off for a good semester together, if I worked hard at it and didn't let a bunch of tough kids do me in.

Chapter Thirty-seven

Facing
Reality

The first weekend after I moved to Seattle and started feeling like a real wife, I found out why Floyd always had to be back in Seattle on Sunday evenings. He took me downtown and introduced me to his dancing friends at the Swedish Club. State liquor laws forbade clubs to serve alcohol on Sundays, so the Swedish Club provided the live music and opened their dance floor to any young people who wanted to do Swedish folk dancing. On Thursdays we also danced at the Norselander, a fine restaurant with a dance floor on their lower level. It was a lot of fun, especially when a Scandinavian ship was in port and sailors were looking for some good clean entertainment. I was fair, with reddish blond hair. If I didn't open my mouth they thought I was a Swede also!

At Floyd's insistence we didn't tell anyone that we were married. I found out that in keeping with his definition of open marriage, he had been dating girls from the folk dance club and he probably dated girls from his classes at the university, even after we were married and I was alone in Aberdeen.

When I found out what had been going on, of course, I was really hurt. Privately, I sobbed and I prayed, and I pleaded and I cried. *Dear Lord, what have I gotten myself into? What can I do about it?*

No point in asking You to change Floyd. I'd never trust him again if You <u>did</u>! That's just the way he is. Me? Should I storm out of this marriage and admit defeat? Can I just hang in there, go with the flow, hope things will get better? God, I don't know what to do. Just please protect me, Lord, if we get into a big fight. Protect me from Floyd if he gets really angry at me? Help me avoid that at all costs!

After sitting home alone, all by myself while Floyd stepped out without me, I made up my mind. I knew Floyd didn't intend to change despite my pleading with him. I wasn't at all happy or approving about the arrangement, but since it didn't include "open sex" on my part, I decided to call his bluff, to get even, to see if he really believed in the equality of our freedom in an open marriage, as he claimed. I wanted to see if he would be jealous. He was. I accepted a date with a fellow from the Swedish Club. When the guy came to pick me up, Floyd hadn't yet left the apartment for the evening. My date knocked on the door. Floyd jumped up and got to the door before me. I had to introduce him to Floyd. Floyd snarled a greeting, letting his anger show. I gave my date no explanation. I didn't expect him to understand any more than I did. I figured that in his eyes, it was better if he thought Floyd and I were merely roommates. The fellow never called for another date.

I knew my personal life was in shambles. It was in direct opposition to all the values I believed in. I was on a self-destructive path. I broke God's commandments and I was guilty before Him. I realized that this wasn't a marriage. I didn't know what it was; only that Floyd had not made the commitment to me that I had expected. I knew there was nothing I could do to change it. We fought and argued all of the time. In only a few months the challenge of the chase was over for him. As for me, our marriage was over too. I decided to leave him. Floyd didn't even object.

A widow, Mrs. Dodge and her wheel-chair- bound adult daughter, Charlotte owned an old, well-kept Victorian in West Seattle, situated high on the crest above the bay. They decided to help with their expenses by renting out a large upstairs bedroom. I became the lucky tenant. My room had huge windows facing the sunrise with a great view, overlooking Elliot Bay and all of downtown Seattle. As I graded papers in the evening at my table in front of one of the windows, I watched the firefly-like lights dancing on the hills across the bay. I felt like I was in Paradise.

Thank God that is over, at last. I've put all of the agony of Floyd behind me. Oh, we'll still see each other at folk dancing every week, but we will ignore each other there just as we've always done. I can handle that. There's no way I am going to let him keep me from enjoying dancing at the Swedish Club!

And so, I turned over a clean page in my book of life. I'd be going home in June. I only had four months to enjoy Seattle and I was determined to make the most of it.

Chapter Thirty-eight

The
Phone Call

While I was teaching one morning, my principal sent me a note saying that he wanted to see me during my lunch period. When I appeared, standing in front of his desk with a sense of impending doom, he asked me,

"Barbara, how long it has it been since you contacted your mother and father?"

With a deep blush I almost whispered,

"More than three or four months, before Floyd and I were married."

"Well, they have been very worried about you. They declared you a missing person. The police in Aberdeen just traced you to this school. "

I was speechless with shame. He asked for no explanation. He just handed me the phone and said,

"I suggest that you call them right now, and promise to call them again this evening."

With that he walked out of his office, leaving me with a phone that seemed to be like a red hot ear muff.

I was floored, and shame overwhelmed me when I realized some of the agony that I had dealt my mom and dad. They probably had been worried about my physical safety. For all they knew, maybe my body was lying in a ditch somewhere…

I did as my principal told me to do.

I dialed that number I knew so well.

"Hello?"

"Hi, Mom. It's…"

"Oh, Bobbie, Thank God, you're still alive!"

Through wrenching sobs, I said,

"Yes, Mom. I'm OK. Is Dad home?"

My mother was crying in relief and I felt I would die in agony and shame.

"No, Dear. He's at work but I'll…"

"Mom? I…I'm terribly sorry I made you worry like this."

"How did you…"

"The police tracked me down. I'm in my principal's office right now. I can't talk long. Please tell Dad that I'll call later this evening and tell you two all about it."

"OK, Honey. We love you so."

"I love you too, Mom. More than you'll ever know. And goodbye for now."

"Goodbye, Dear. We'll be waiting for your call."

I hung up and dissolved in the tears that I had been trying to control. After a few minutes I struggled to regain my composure. I had a classroom full of kids to deal with in just about a half hour. I powdered my nose and my red eyes. Instead of facing anyone in the lounge, I skipped lunch and went back to my classroom to get myself in shape and ready for the return of my students.

That evening I bought a fist full of quarters to use on a payphone so I could call Mom and Dad in the complete privacy of a phone booth. I told them the whole sorry mess. I reassured them by telling them that I had left Floyd and was living by myself in West Seattle. They told me they would always love me, and that I could come home again as soon as school was out in June.

Just as it had been back at Glen Park School in Gary, when my whole world turned upside down, and I seemed to be tossed violently in whitewater rapids, I didn't drown because I had a sanctuary. I knew that in spite of it all, that God would protect me and that my parents and my classroom were my life raft. In my classroom I could block out all thoughts of disaster at home and concentrate on my responsibilities. My students' well-being and progress was my mission, and their respect and love gave me another life.

I was also able to separate my emotional turmoil from the beauty and enjoyment of Seattle. It was all mine. I loved the cool, temperate climate, the lovely neighborhoods carpeting the hills and ridges surrounding the bay and harbor, and the sparkling lights on those hills at night. On my way home in the evening I enjoyed taking time out of my bus transfer downtown to go shopping in Pike Place Market and bringing home fresh fish and vegetables for dinner. I even loved the rain. Like a heavy mist, it freshened my makeup in the morning. Mild sunshine waited for me almost every afternoon as I came home from school, wearing a sweater and carrying my raincoat. Above all, I loved the year round greenery, the busy harbor, and the blue water of Seattle's bay and lakes. The city too was a sanctuary and no evil would ever sully my memories of it.

An old hymn seemed to really speak to me when I was struggling against Floyd's influence over my personal life. I didn't fully understand the importance of verse three at that time, but I loved the song anyway, even though I was still denying the deity of Jesus Christ.

LOVE LIFTETH ME

Words by James Rowe, 1912
Music by Howard E. Smith

I was sinking deep in sin, far from the peaceful shore,
Very deeply stained within, sinking to rise no more,
But the Master of the sea, heard my despairing cry,
From the waters lifted me, now safe am I.

Refrain:

Love lifteth me! Love lifteth me!
When nothing else could help
Love lifteth me!

All my heart to him I give, ever to Him I'll cling.
In His blessed presence live, ever His praises sing,
Love so mighty and so true, Merits my soul's best songs,
Faithful, loving service too, to Him belongs.

Refrain

Souls in danger look above, Jesus completely saves,
He will lift you by His love, out of the angry waves.
He's the Master of the sea, billows His will obey,
He your Savior wants to be. Be saved today.

Love lifteth me! Love lifteth me!
When nothing else could help,
Love lifteth me!

Chapter Thirty-nine

Suicides?

After I left Floyd and moved to West Seattle, I continued to go to the Swedish Club for folk dancing. Although we seldom spoke to each other, Floyd came to the dances, too. About a month after I moved out on him, as he put it, I noticed that he was looking more and more disheveled. He never had been good-looking or dashing but had been neat to a fault. Now he had dark circles under his eyes, his unshaven scraggly bristles of a beard stood in stark, dirty contrast to his sallow complexion and hollow cheeks.

I wonder what's wrong with Floyd. He was always so fastidious about his appearance. Now he looks like he only shaves once in a while, if he feels like it! And, he needs a haircut. So unlike him.

I couldn't help but stare at him whenever I passed him in our circle dancing. Later, during intermission, I was sitting on one of the folding chairs that ring the edge of the big ballroom floor, when I saw him heading toward me. I smiled and nodded to him and he took it as an invitation to join me. He slumped into the empty chair beside me.

He reached for my outstretched hand and said, "Oh, Bonnie, I need to talk to you."

How I hate that name! He had no right to rename me! He doesn't own me any more!

"Bonnie, you have no idea how much I still love you, even after you treated me so bad. I'm simply devastated without you. I'm so lonely I can hardly stand it."

I gently withdrew my hand from his clammy grasp.

"Why are you lonely? You have your classes at the university and some of the girls there to keep you busy."

"No, I don't. Even though I'm an adult, they sent my grade records to my dad. He found out that I was only taking a few isolated classes rather than in a program leading to a degree, and besides my grades weren't good enough for him. All of the turmoil I've been in because of you! I couldn't concentrate on my studies. Anyway, he cut me off!"

"Oh, I'm sorry Floyd."

"I had to sell my car and I'm behind on my rent. I'll never catch up. I don't know what I'm going to do."

"Well, you can always go back home and work for your dad."

"And leave you here all by yourself? I couldn't ever do that, Bonnie. Anyway, I don't have any money for the plane ticket."

"Well, neither do I. And, please don't call me that any more. I am not your little Bonnie. My name is Barbara to anyone outside my family, including you…"

"So, it has come to that? I'm just a friend, not family?"

"You never were a part of my family. You deliberately turned them against you from the beginning."

"I can't help it if your mother and father never liked me," he whined as he brushed his uncombed hair back from his eyes.

I took a deep breath and almost hissed in my effort to show anger and yet not attract attention of people around us.

"You isolated me from everyone in your effort to control me. Thank God, you had to depend on my teaching or you would've ruined that, too."

In despair, he groped for my hand again.

"Now Bonnie, you know that isn't true. Your dedication to your teaching was the only… I mean that's the place where I respected you the most…"

"That's right, that's the only place you've shown any respect for me…"

"Besides I was just trying to build a marriage where we loved each other so much that we didn't need anyone else. That's real togetherness"

"Well, that's your opinion! I call it domination and control. It's not for me! Never again."

I'm getting embarrassed for fear others are overhearing our "conversation". Oh, good, time to get up and dance. Saved by the music!

During the next week, Floyd called me every evening on Mrs. Dodge's telephone. It was apparent he was in trouble, mentally, and financially. He just couldn't cope. I told Mrs. Dodge about it because I was beginning to see what was going to follow.

"Now, Barbara, we know you're still married… If moving in with you rather than being kicked out on the streets becomes necessary, I won't object. I hope for your sake it'll only be a temporary situation."

Floyd begged me to take him back. He tried to convince me that he was abject and beaten because of losing me, that he desperately needed my tender, loving care and that we should try again to make a go of our marriage. He sounded so weak and helpless. I winced every time I thought about him and eventually I began to feel responsible for his misery, just as he intended.

Feeling guilty, with Mrs. Dodge's permission, out of what I thought was compassion, not love, I let him move in with me one more time. Of course, that led me to recreating my own personal Hell at home. And I realized that I remained firmly ensnared in Floyd's clutches, whenever he chose to claim me.

Shortly afterward, as I rode the bus home after school one evening, my thoughts turned to the mess I was in with Floyd.

When I divorced Johnny I figured it all out as completely his fault. Now I have to face some facts:

Why do I think of myself as the innocent one in two failed marriages?

What had gone wrong, not only once, but twice?

Why did I make such poor choices in dating to begin with?

Why did I let myself get involved sexually? Doesn't that cloud my thinking about the wisdom of getting married?

I'm not sour on marriage. I know there is still someone else out there for me. I don't want to blow it all over again.

I knew I had to make sure I wouldn't make the same mistakes in the future. I was confused about everything involved in my relationship with Floyd, even back to the initial attraction I felt for him. It sure wasn't because he was dashing or good looking, because he actually was rather mousy looking with his beady blue eyes and slight build. I had to admit that it was sex, pure and simple.

Tears began to trickle over my cheeks. I sniffed, hunted for my hankie, and dabbed at my eyes. I decided to face up to reality once more.

The next day I screwed up my courage and asked my principal for a recommendation for a psychologist that could help me deal with marital problems. I went to his recommended clinic and filled out the required pen and paper questionnaire. I frowned and protested to the interviewer when I was told a woman would be assigned to me. I wanted a man as my counselor.

Maybe a man will take my desperate complaints against Floyd at face value. A woman would force me to dig deeper into my motives... No, that's not it. The truth is I still want to try to impress men and a woman would see though my motives.

I knew that I needed help, but I didn't yet want to reveal the inner me to anyone else. My request was not granted and I was assigned to a female counselor. She seemed cold and impersonal.

The counselors in the clinic practiced non-directional counseling. My counselor never asked me any questions or probed but let me just talk about anything I wanted. I mentally rehearsed all week before seeing her as to what part of my life I would tell her about this time. I tried to avoid digging into my present situation. I hoped that when she knew all about my past, she would then be able to tell me what to do next. But I couldn't stick to telling her only about my past. Time after time I ended up crying about my misery in being married to Floyd. The result was that it got more and more difficult, after ripping Floyd up one side and down the other in every session, to pick up carry-out dinners and go back to my room and to a man that I had come to loath. I never did get any outright advice from her but it became apparent to me that my so-called marriage put me in an impossible position that I had to get out of as soon as possible.

One night as I stood outside the clinic offices in the early evening, waiting for a bus to go home, I thought about what I should do to get out of the mess I had let Floyd create for me. I was still blaming him for everything. And why, most of all, had I been so vulnerable to his charms in what seemed so long ago?

*So here I am! I hate him, I hate him, I **hate** him. Why am I standing here? Why am I going home to him? Is there really any solution? How am I going to get free?*

As I stood there on the corner, all wrapped up in my agony, I was oblivious to others waiting with me. I absently watched cars make right hand turns just a few feet in front of us. We all had to scramble backwards like frightened crabs when one driver, in a hurry, cut the corner too closely and almost jumped the curb.

Wow, that was a close one! I wasn't the only one who was afraid of getting hit! We could have all been smashed against that wall behind us!

What would happen if I stepped off of the curb just as a car turned in front of me?.... I'd get smashed good! Maybe if I just kinda fell under the front wheel?.... Funny, that doesn't scare me at all. It would all be over so soon, it wouldn't even hurt!... Let's see... I have to make sure the driver is a man... But not that one. That was a woman driving...And so was that one... I can't see the driver from here,...Is this one coming a man?... No, I can't tell until the car is right in front of me, too late to jump...

I really thought seriously about suicide but I guess God had other plans for me. My alibi for not following through was because there was no way I could tell ahead of time if the driver was a man or a woman. I rationalized that if I did decide to do it, I had to be sure I threw myself in front of a man, just to get even with THEM. THEY had it coming. In no way would I jump in front of a woman, because she had more than enough troubles herself, because of men, and she didn't need me messing up *her* life, too!

Floyd did nothing all day but wallow around in bed, unshaven, unkempt and even unwashed. He was in such a deep depression that it got so that I actually rushed home each lunch hour to see if he was still alive. When I raced up the stairs to my room, I clenched my hands and held my breath. I envisioned him lying in a blood soaked bed, with a horrible oozing hole in his head, dead of a gunshot wound from his own gun.

That fear, *or hope!?* never materialized. I thought the real solution was for Floyd to call his father and ask for a one-way plane ticket home. After much pleading and attempts to reason with him in the evenings, I finally threatened to call his dad myself. At last, he called his dad, the ticket came through, he let me take him to the airport and I sent him out of my life forever.

Part Five

Impaled, Interlude

And after you have suffered
for a little while,
the God of all grace,
who called you to His eternal glory
in Christ, will Himself
perfect, confirm, strengthen,
and establish you.

1 Peter 5: 10 NAS

Chapter Forty

Sue Takahashi

...And life went on, blissfully, and thankfully, without Floyd Dubois to mess it (and me) up! But I was to enjoy it for only a brief three months!

My best friend in Seattle became Sue Takahashi, the little Japanese teacher whose classroom was across the hall from mine. We were both young, less experienced teachers and had a lot of fun sharing tales of our teaching efforts and the shenanigans of our kids. Sometimes when we were alone, I encouraged Sue to tell me what it was like to be Japanese in our Caucasian society. Only once did she tell of her life during World War II, and that was a long intense story. I never wanted to put her through that again. She said Seattle seemed to have a collective guilt about how the Japanese Americans were treated during the war and she didn't want to be critical or embarrass anyone.

We were eating dinner together after school in a small café near our bus transfer point. It was early and not many customers had come in yet. We had a quiet, more private booth back in a far corner. My intellectual curiosity forced me to open up a sensitive topic that I was afraid would be painful to both of us, but I knew our friendship was strong and one built on trust and honesty. It would survive.

Sue took a deep breath and said,

"Well, you know, I was just a teenager when the War (II) started. My parents owned our house and a successful restaurant in 'Japantown', here in Seattle. My father was a good business man and he saw serious trouble ahead with the Japanese, even before Pearl Harbor. Late in 1941 he sold our house for a fairly good price and put the money in a western bank, not a local Japanese one. He moved Mom, my younger brother and me into a rented flat. After we declared war on Japan, the bottom dropped out on all Japanese properties; homes, apartment buildings, businesses, and even farm land. The westerners knew we would be forced to move and abandon everything and they bought up whatever they wanted, at terrible discounts, from the desperate Japanese owners."

Tears began to fill her eyes, but she paused and then almost whispered,

"The fear and hatred of the westerners toward us had always been present but after Pearl Harbor, it simply exploded. The westerners said 'dirty little Japs' right to our faces!"

I shook my head, looked downcast, and sighed to show sympathy.

"Yes, I read about it in the paper and heard about it on the radio. The government and people were really in a panic."

Sue frowned and gulped. Maybe repressed memories were tumbling back on her? She looked around to check on our privacy before she responded in a lowered voice.

"You wouldn't believe what was going on out here all up and down the coast. The FBI considered all of us as possible 'enemy aliens'. We never knew when the police might swoop down, into our businesses and even our homes, looking for any evidence that someone was a spy or a saboteur. If they found any forbidden communication equipment like radio transmitters, shortwave radios, special cameras, that was enough evidence to condemn anyone."

"How horrible! You must have been really afraid."

Her brow cleared and she nodded her head.

"But you know, some of their fear was justified. There really were a large bunch of Japanese enemy aliens who were organized and working toward violent overthrow of the local government and sabotage against critical facilities. They were looking forward to the Japanese invasion of our country! There wasn't any obvious way for the public to judge. Everyone was afraid that the Japanese really were going to invade the West Coast and that the westerners couldn't trust anyone with yellow skin and almond eyes. They had no way of sorting out all of us who were loyal Americans from the possible spies and collaborators, so they just had to get all Japanese away from the coast."

"You're defending the government! How about you? Did you really experience that hatred yourself?"

"No, because I tried to be invisible. I obeyed all of the rules that they set up to protect themselves from us. I didn't try to use any public transportation. I didn't do any shopping outside of Japantown. We all, even my dad, made sure we were at home before the 9:00 curfew. My father had one of his employees drive us back and forth to school. We even heard about a principal somewhere who went out and picked up his Japanese students in his own car and brought them to school because they weren't allowed to use the public buses. There were some westerners who were kind and concerned about us, especially our principal and our teachers."

I realized I wanted to hear some kind of anger or desire to retaliate from her and so I continued to probe.

"I read in the paper that in LA when they wanted to clear the Japanese out of 'Little Tokyo' they declared it a slum area and forced everyone to move out."

Leaning forward with intensity and in that soft voice, she said,

"Of course, Barbara, some of our areas were kind of slummy because we had been discriminated against for long before the war, ever since we arrived as immigrants. It was very hard to secure good paying jobs outside of our own community. After Pearl Harbor the government tried to get us to voluntarily move into the interior of the country. Some of us who had relatives in the South and Midwest did pull out, but most Nisei didn't have the resources to make the move."

"Nisei? Who are the Nisei?"

"I am Nicei. Our young men in the army over in Europe were Nisei...The second generation, born here in America. Our property became almost worthless. My father tried to sell his restaurant but finally succeeded selling it as a short sale at far, far below what it was worth. He sold the furniture and fixtures at ten cents on the dollar. He was heart broken."

"But he didn't move you voluntarily?"

I felt apologetic about probing into family finances and personal matters but I really wanted to understand and feel her pain.

"No, no place to go. He didn't have any contacts outside of Seattle and he felt he had to conserve what little resources he had managed to save. By the middle of March, Congress authorized the evacuation as mandatory. Notices were put up on lamp posts and bulletin boards announcing the date when we had to report to the fairgrounds of Puyallup, a town about 25 miles southeast of here. It was our assigned assembly center."

"Didn't I see some horrible pictures of people being loaded up into buses?" I said.

"Yes, and they lugged along all they could carry, trunks, suitcases, and bundles of clothes and valuables. We were luckier. My father had western friends who let him store household things with them and one of them drove us to Puyallup."

"You had to live in tents there, didn't you?"

"No, but thousands of us lived for about three months in so-called barracks made out of animal stalls and the girders under the grandstands. There weren't enough government issued mattresses so some people slept on canvas bags stuffed with straw. But I think one of the worst things for me was the embarrassment, the indignity of sharing living areas and toilets and bathing facilities."

"I know that was bad. I've always thought of the Japanese as very private people, especially the women. Remember how your mother wouldn't even let you stay over night with me after a PTA meeting because a girl or young woman always sleeps under her parent's roof until married?"

"Yes, and it's amazing how strong those traditions persisted even under the worst of living conditions, or maybe it was because of those bad conditions?."

"And, in good times, too. Cultural traditions are so powerful, aren't they? Were the relocation camps really bad?"

Again Sue looked around to check on our privacy, but the waitress brought our dinners to us and she continued after we were all settled down and eating our diner.

Chapter Forty-one

Camp Minidoka

I resumed our conversation by asking Sue, "Weren't living conditions almost impossible for the Japanese in the internment camps?"

Smiling only briefly, she said, "Yes, but things were a little bit better when we Japanese Americans were taken to Camp Minidoka in Idaho, even if the weather was horrible. There we found 500 separate barracks, but they were made of tar paper stretched over wooden frames! And we lived in these "shelters" even in below zero temperatures during the winter! We were grateful for wooden floors this time even if the grass grew up in the cracks between the planks in the spring. Our whole family was allotted only one room, about 20 x 24 feet. No plumbing or cooking facilities, only one army cot per person with blankets and a small stove for heating. We had to go outside to toilets, showers, and a washhouse in the center of each complex. That building served about 250 people."

"Again, no privacy!"

Again she surprised me with her attitude when she added,

"But you know, Barbara, living like that was a part of our war effort. We knew that we were living just like, or even better than, a lot of our boys in the service, and we would survive. We ate in mess halls and the children played in the dust, the mud, and the snow.

Sometimes the thermometers fell to ten to twenty degrees below zero, but in the summer it got up to 110 to 115 degrees!"

"And, Sue, you were used to the mild weather of Seattle! Did you have any opportunity to buy things that you needed like cold weather clothes?"

"I didn't hear of anyone freezing to death! The government hired as many of our people as possible, at very low wages, to run the camp; cooks, police, doctors, nurses, school teachers, maintenance workers, etc. My mother and father worked as cooks in one of the cafeterias, so we had some money to buy necessities from a very limited commissary. Some people who were able to get very strict security clearance were even permitted to work outside, "over the fence." So we had some money to buy necessities. After all, we were fighting a war and everyone in the country had to cut back as a part of our war effort.

"You know, Barbara, I've been thinking as I talk to you, maybe in one sense the government was protecting us from all of the anger and hatred that gripped the country. I guess our military had to build up extreme hatred in the army to get their soldiers to kill other men like they had to do."

"But that hatred was all over the country, not just in the army."

Sue replied, "That hatred was part of fighting the war on the home front, of mobilizing everyone to support our troops. But the worst thing is when they lumped all of us together and called us 'dirty little Japs.'"

There! She used that name again! I guess that really hurt.

Sue responded to my interest in a far more tolerant manner than I expected. I was surprised at some of her rationalizing in defense of <u>her</u> government. I wondered if the teachers in the camps fed that sense of patriotic loyalty in the students, despite how poorly they were being treated. But I didn't get a chance to ask . Her story was winding down and I didn't want to interrupt her.

"After the war they brought us home to Seattle. We had no claim to anything, not our homes or our businesses. We had to start all over. It was too much for my father. He died of a heart attack and left my mother with my brother and me to feed. We were lucky again because Mother still had some of the money that Dad had deposited in that bank before we had to leave Seattle.

She moved us into a government housing project and I obtained scholarships so that I could go to college and get my teachers' license."

"Sue, I can't believe that you don't seem as bitter as I expected about the way the Japanese Americans were treated during the war."

"Well, my mom is still bitter. But her generation lost so much more than mine. For the Nisei, that was just our normal childhood, not our adulthood. When the war was over, we were free and the whole world lay before us, prejudice and all. And we <u>had </u>learned how to cope.

"And so here I am and-I love being a school teacher," she said with pride and not a hint of bitterness.

Chapter Forty-two

Japanese Americans

SEATTLE, 1953

Since I was free from Floyd's control, it didn't take me long to set up a full social schedule. One of my favorite activities was to go out to dinner with Sue and her fiancé, Riku. He was a graduate student and so they didn't object too much to me picking up my part of the check most of the time. Even then, I felt an indebtedness and said that the next time the dinner was on me. I wanted to make it a party, to celebrate our friendship and Sue's kindness to me. I intended to choose the place, make the reservations, and pick up the tab. But later, in privacy, Sue protested, and I resisted. She finally confessed,

"Riku thinks he should make the reservation because... ah,... there are still some places ...ah,... that refuse to serve us!"

"Oh, no! I didn't realize ...The war was a long time ago! ... I can't believe ... This is 1953! ...I thought that by now everyone understood and felt sympathy, not prejudice, for the Japanese Americans!"

"That's OK, Barbara. We live with it all the time and we're used to it!"

I sighed in embarrassment and disappointment.

"Well, please tell Riku that I apologize for putting both of you in this position. I'll be very happy to be hostess for our dinner wherever he chooses. I know the food will be great."

Sue and I became such good friends that she invited me to spend a Sunday afternoon with her in her mother's apartment in "The Project."(government housing for those with lower incomes) It was a special Japanese holiday and I was very honored to be included in a small family celebration that included her brother who was home from college for the weekend. It would be a special occasion and she said Mother would be making "sooshi" or something like that.

I stood in the little kitchen and watched Mrs. Takahashi work. She did everything with big wooden chopsticks the size of your finger. She handled liquids with wooden paddles and ladles. With her kitchen chopsticks she unwrapped a bundle of sheets of grayish green dried sea weed. They were so thin they were translucent and very crisp. Still using her chopsticks, not her fingers, she held the first one over the gas flames on her stove until it got soft and pliable. She spread it out on her cutting board and covered it with about a quarter inch of cooked white rice. On top of that she laid long strips of some kind of pickled vegetable and long thin spears of big white radishes and mushrooms. Finally, came the "piece d' resistance".

"What's that?" I asked idly. It was long strips of black shiny eel that had been cured in brine!

Oh, No! Not eel! I could never eat eel! … Now, Barbara, you consider yourself an adventurous eater. You know this is a traditional dish that they are serving to honor Lillian's brother. It's a big deal! And you are honored to be included! You simply can't insult them! But EEL? OH, YUCK! How will I ever be able to choke it down?

Mrs. Takahashi, still with only her chopsticks, carefully picked up the edges of the sea weed and formed everything into a roll about an inch and a half in diameter. She pushed it aside to 'rest' and began to make other rolls with different combinations of steamed greens, cooked or pickled vegetables, mushrooms, cooked egg, pork, ham and ...

Oops! ... Whoopee do! ... RAW FISH? It looks like thin slices of salmon, or is it tuna? ... Well, I guess that's not so bad. I like smoked salmon on my cream cheese and bagel, don't I? ... Somehow that's not nearly as bad as EEL! I had better quit shivering about shooshi. I AM going to eat it regardless, aren't I?

When Mrs. Takahashi sliced the rolls and arranged them on plain white platters, they looked so pretty...like desserts, in fact! She smiled with pride in her creativity. We sat down in the cozy dining room in a festive mood. We laughed at the teasing banter between Sue and her brother as we ate a meal of cold shooshi (sushi!) and hot tea. The eel tasted salty, the salmon was good, and everything else was delicious. I, was proud, ... that I had passed the biggest cultural sensitivity test of my life, so far!

Chapter Forty-three

The New "Me"

Early spring of 1953 in Seattle brought out a brand new me. I thrived in my freedom from Floyd's influence. I enjoyed the challenge of trying to stay on top of some really unruly kids in my classroom and I was thrilled as spring flowers began to pop out in the balmy weather. I felt like I was a kind of spring flower myself. This was the Seattle I had dreamed about. In addition to my friendships at school, I was having a literal ball at the Swedish Club every Sunday evening. True, before I sent Floyd home to his Dad, he was there too, but I was used to ignoring him there, since Floyd insisted in acting like we weren't married. That was really easy then, but even better when he no longer was breathing down my neck.

One of the reasons Swedish folk dancing was so much fun was that there was very little emphasis on pairing up or dating. The only reason a fellow asked a girl to dance with him was because we had to be sure there was an equal number of both guys and gals. I never had to suffer as a wallflower because pairing up entailed no commitment to romance or cuddling. Just pure clean fun for everyone. It had some of the same qualities as square dancing only it was done in one great big circle.

When the music started, the couples bowed to each other and went through a prescribed dancing pattern that lasted only a minute or two. As the girls turned out of the circle in solo little whirls, all of the fellows moved forward one space to their new partner. As the girls twirled back into the circle, they found new men waiting for them. The new pairs greeted each other with smiles, curtsies or bows, and repeated the set pattern until time for another partner change.

The dances were exciting, lovely, graceful, and very friendly mixers. The Varso Vienna (a waltz) and the Swedish schottische (far more vigorous) were my favorites. In this relaxed atmosphere it was easy to make friends and to get together afterwards at the corner ice cream shop to "recover from all of the exercise!" That's where I learned about strawberry waffles with fresh berries, rimmed with a fluffy wall of whipped cream, to the dismay of my waistline!

Chapter Forty-four

Dungeness Crab

One of the men I enjoyed visiting with at folk dancing was Bill Jones. He was rather like an unpolished gemstone, rough around the edges but intriguing inside. He was an amateur sailor and loved the water, just as I did. As we relaxed in the ice cream shop one evening, he said,

"How about it, Barbara? Let me show you how we eat crab in Seattle."

Dungeness crab was in season and I had tasted that delicacy only once before.

"That sounds great! I'm very adventuresome when it comes to food. I know I'll love it."

"I'll pick you up on Saturday and we'll drive down the coast a ways and find ourselves some crab."

We enjoyed a beautiful day on our way south. There were a few fish shacks scattered along the road. Finally, we stopped at one of the shacks and Bill picked out the biggest crab in the bunch. They were a bright pink because they had already been cooked in a big cauldron of boiling water. He paid for it along with a little cup of catsup mixed with horseradish for dipping, a small stack of soda crackers, and two bottles of pop. (That's 'Midwestern' for sodas like Pepsi, Coke, and Orange Crush.) He asked them to wrap the crab up in a lot of newspapers and they gave us a handful of paper napkins and a couple of meat skewers.

This looks like fun! I wonder where we are going to eat. It's going to be too messy to eat in his car even if it is an old clunker!

Bill found a shady picnic table in a roadside park overlooking Puget Sound. He spread the newspaper out on the table. I followed his example. We cracked the shells with our teeth, ate with our fingers and pulled the meat out of the smaller claws with our skewers. We made a big mess, laughing all the time. The crab was delicious. As we were cleaning up, Bill assumed a serious expression.

THE CLUNKER

"Barbara, I've decided to join the merchant marines."

Well, there goes that romance! It's obvious I'm not very important to him!

"Oh, that's great, Bill. But we'll all miss you at the Swedish Club. It sounds like you'll get a chance to travel, won't you?"

"That's right. But I want to make a deal with you. If you will take me down to the docks next Saturday morning, I'll let you use my car until you go home to Indiana in June."

"Oh, that's wonderful, Bill. I'll be able to explore Seattle on my own and really soak it up."

"Well, you know the car isn't much. The starter gets disengaged every once in a while and I haven't been able to find that short in the horn, but it runs good. I don't think you will have any trouble with it."

"But if I do have trouble?"

"I'll give you my brother's phone number and he'll come and get it. In fact, when you get ready to go back home, you can call him and he will take you to the airport in it and then take it home to keep for me."

"Oh, I'm so excited. Thank you, thank you, and thank you!"

Outa My Way!

My first real jaunt in "my" clunker was to take Sue downtown to Nordstrom's (a very nice department store) after school. What an adventure that was! The traffic on the main road around the north end of the bay was horrible.

"You know, Sue, I have a theory about this traffic."

"What is it?"

"Well, on the days that everyone is speeding and zipping around each other, switching lanes and so forth, those are the same days that our kids are antsy and hyper in the classroom."

"Really? I wonder why? What's the connection?"

"I haven't been able to figure that one out. It isn't because of rain…I wonder if air pressure has anything to do with it? Or an impending storm?"

"I don't know but it's fun to think about. Let's see if both your kids and mine are hyper on the same days."

As we left the highway and came into the downtown area, I warned,

"OK, now hold on to your hat. So far I haven't had to make a right hand turn. When I do, the horn will blare all the way around the corner! Now we have to look for a parking place."

"This is going to be fun!"

I drove around in left hand circles looking for a spot, with no luck. We didn't want to have to pay a parking fee in a lot. When I got down to the waterfront and couldn't make another left turn, I said,

"Watch this! Here we go!"

The minute I turned the steering wheel to the right, the horn started blowing, warning everyone that I was coming through.

"Hey, did you see that little old lady jump back up on the curb as though she thought I was going to run her down? Whee! What a kick!"

After that whenever I had to turn right, I grinned and put my hands up high on the steering wheel where, hopefully, people could see that I wasn't deliberately rushing them with all of that racket. Then I looked over at my little Japanese friend. She had shrunk down into her seat, out of sight, in sheer embarrassment. Her face was a burnished copper!

About that time it happened! The car died out, thankfully on a side street, but in downtown Seattle. I couldn't get the motor to even turn over. Before Sue could panic, I said, "Never mind, Bill never told me how to fix it, but it seems to be something simple and obvious to most men. Watch me see how soon we can get some help."

I got out of the car, propped up the hood, and leaned over the front fender with one high heel held high in the air, as though I was straining to reach something. The first car to pass us came to a screeching halt. The man came back to ask if he could help. I told him what I thought was wrong and in just a few minutes he had us on our way!

I decided that was enough games for awhile and pulled into a parking garage. As we walked away we could hear the horn sounding off all the way up as the valet parked my clunker on the top floor. We giggled and pretended we were mystified by the disruption just like everyone else.

Chapter Forty-five

The Other "Me"

One morning after several months of teaching in Seattle, I was deep into a math lesson. I heard the rear door to my classroom open ever so carefully. I looked up in curiosity. I stiffened and my room suddenly seemed far too warm. My supervisor 'dropped in' to observe me and write up a report! She slipped into a desk in the back of the room.

I was told to expect her someday, but that only added to my anxiety! Why today? During a math lesson, of all things?

I gulped in surprise, and dismay. She apparently didn't want to be recognized or to interrupt my teaching. I had no choice but to go with the lesson as if she wasn't there. As I wrote on the blackboard the chalk dust choked me up at first and my voice sounded deep and scratchy, but I soon got back in stride.

It was obvious to her, I hoped, that the kids wanted my attention and approval because they not only raised their hands to my questions, some of them even waved them. They weren't ashamed of appearing eager as they were when I first took over the class. They were alert and engaged. I was proud of them.

But then, things began to fall apart. Bill sent a note up the aisle. We all knew that it was going to Angie. Probably about plans for lunch. Then Hector, in the back of the room, dropped all of his lunch money change and everyone around him scrambled to help him retrieve it.

I was losing them, but I never raised my voice. Instead I pulled my Mattie Hahnz trick again until I had their attention. The tantalizing fragrance of sloppy joes wafted up from the cafeteria. I couldn't compete with rumbling hunger pangs. In a softer voice I closed off the lesson and told them to put their things away.

I picked up a well worn teal-blue book that was always handy on my desk. I stood quietly and smiled until they settled down. When they saw me open my poetry book to a badly smudged page, they gave me their full attention in anticipation of what they knew was to come. In a booming voice, I launched into,

"Ho! For the Pirate Don Dirk of Dowdee,

For he is as wicked as wicked can be."

In a softer, simpering voice, and rolling my eyes, I recited,

"But, oh, he was simply gorgeous to see,

Was the Pirate Don Dirk of Dowdee."

I really hammed it up and before I had finished the poem, they were eating out of my hands. I continued to read or recite other favorite poems for them for the six or eight minutes until the lunch bell rang. We were all in good spirits as they filed out of the room and I turned to greet my supervisor. She shook my hand and thanked me for a most enjoyable visit.

Several days later I received a copy of her report. She said the math lesson was well presented but she began to worry when I lost their attention just before lunch. Then her heart dropped when she saw me pick up my Arbuthnot poetry book!

Oh, no! She's not going to try to read poetry to this group of roughnecks, not now!

To her surprise, they settled down right away, in anticipation! Those tough kids actually enjoyed poetry! She said it only proved her theory that a teacher can 'sell' anything that she herself loves. She marked me as "surpassing district standards". I guess I came out smelling like a rose, a very fragrant "Mr. Lincoln" rose, that is! Thanks to Mattie Hahnz and <u>*her*</u> love of poetry!

So much for grieving around about Floyd Dubois! Who needs him?

Chapter Forty-six

Happy Birthday!

MAY 29, 1953

It was a tradition at school to bring your own birthday cake to share with everyone in the teachers' lounge. Although cooking in Mrs. Dodge's kitchen wasn't a part of our verbal contract, I wanted to take my famous shaved chocolate cake when my birthday rolled around in May. I would never take a store-bought anything to any party. I cherished my reputation as a good cook. I asked Mrs. Dodge for special permission to bake a cake in her kitchen. Of course, she said "OK".

After eating dinner and shopping on my way home, I assembled the ingredients for the cake. I turned the oven on to preheat. I carefully folded egg yolks and dry ingredients into the stiffly beaten egg whites, spooned the fluffy batter into the borrowed angel food cake pan and slid it into the hot oven. I wiped beads of sweat from my forehead. I set the timer for 40 minutes and went upstairs to grade papers while the cake baked. By then it was almost nine o'clock at night. At 9:40 I returned to the kitchen to check to see if my cake was done. I stuck a toothpick into it in several places and the tooth pick always came out clean, not gooey. The top of the cake was a bit browner than usual, but no problem.

Boy, is that good timing! I'll let it cool for just a few minutes and then I'll turn it out on a cake plate. As soon as I get the kitchen cleaned up, I'm going to bed. I'm bushed!

When the clean-up chore was done, I got out the borrowed cake plate. I balanced the plate over the exact center of the cake, still in the pan, took a good grip on both of them, and flipped them over.

OH! NO! WHAT HAPPENED? WHAT IS ALL OF THAT GOOP DRIPPING OFF OF THE CABINETS? AND ALL OVER THE STOVE? Stand still! Be careful! It's all over the floor, too!

I had warm, sticky cake batter all over everything! It even dripped from the door handles and ran down the refrigerator door behind me! There on the counter was a one inch layer of baked sponge cake. It was just as thick the length of a poked toothpick! I tried to figure out what had happened. Mrs. Dodge had an electric oven. I was used to a gas one. Her oven had two grills, one up and one down. I had turned on only the upper one! The broiler grill! I was lucky it hadn't burned the top layer! My cake had only cooked down from the top as far as the depth of a poked toothpick, and the rest was yellow, chocolate flaked gravy, now all over someone else's kitchen!

I started scrubbing the kitchen with hot sudsy water and wondered what I should do next. I tried to be very quiet because I didn't want to alert Mrs. Dodge that I was having trouble. Above all, I didn't want her to see what I had done to her kitchen!

I _have_ to have a cake for tomorrow! The bakery won't be open before I have to be in school tomorrow morning. I guess I have no choice but to bake another one right now. Thank goodness I have enough stuff here to do it all over again!

It was midnight before my cake was done and the kitchen was spotless. I crawled up the stairs to my room and into bed, to dream of being carried away in a river of cold yellow gravy, marked with black flakes of burned cake!

At school the next day we celebrated my 24th birthday and my Shaved Chocolate Cake was a big hit, as usual.

Chapter Forty-seven

The Letter Home

Dear Mom and Dad,

I just have to tell you what has been going on out here for me. First, I finally got rid of Floyd for good. He was really sick and very depressed. I sent him on a plane back to his dad. Let them deal with him at home. I'm through.

My teaching is going well. My sixth graders are responding and learning. They're much better, more respectful than when I first came here. I don't know if we've caught up with what they missed the first semester, but we're trying.

The Seattle school district has a very interesting form of in-service education that I know you'll be interested in. Several times a year a half day substitute is sent to cover for a less experienced teacher so that she or he can leave the classroom and observe an assigned 'Master Teacher' at work. My first assignment was to visit Margaret Morgan's class right next door.

One of their activities that morning was to give oral reports and to respond to them. I was impressed with the quality of the reports and the stage presence her students exhibited. Their comments afterward seemed very mature. Then, as Margaret instructed them, I discovered the formula they were following:

After a presentation was completed, each suggestion or question by another student had to be preceded by a complimentary observation. That we all know. It was good to be seeing it taught in the classroom, but what impressed me most was every time a comment was made, the recipient had to indicate verbally that he or she heard what was said. Then the respondent was required to accept each statement verbally and <u>then</u> follow it with at least one full sentence of explanation or information that furthered the discussion.

It was this last part that I was so glad to hear. I thought it was a great lesson because of the application I made to its use in social situations. I taught my students that they had a courteous obligation to always reply to questions with more than just a simple yes or no, but to add a sentence or two every time to keep the conversational ball rolling. It's really is a good social skill to develop.

Now Mom, let me tell you about Margaret Morgan, that Master Teacher next door.

One morning I greeted Sue out in the hall to express my amazement. Our conversation went somewhat like this:

"Margaret is going to be absent again for two weeks! To go on a trip, <u>again!</u>"

Sue explained it to me and it simply blew my mind!

"You see, this is the arrangement under which she agreed to teach. The district recognizes her as such a good teacher that she is permitted to take off any time she pleases!"

Wow! How's that, Dad? But I do agree. She is absolutely great. I've learned so much from her, not only on my observation assignment, but just talking with her in the hall and on our lunch hour.

Sue confided, "I heard our supervisor and principal explain it. They said she was so good that she could teach in one semester what it takes a regular teacher the rest of the year to cover."

Raising my eyebrows, I said, "Isn't that stretching a bit?"

"I suppose so. But her husband is a vice- president of a big airlines and he wants her to be able to travel with him. He said she couldn't go back to teaching unless the district made her travel possible."

I was amazed! "Whatta life! I should be so lucky?... But what about continuity for the students?"

"She notifies the principal ahead of time and makes copious lesson plans. They always send in the same substitute who I assume is a very good teacher, also."

Mom, I decided she really has it made. I just hope that someday I can afford to travel during my summer vacation! In the meantime, I'm really enjoying Seattle. This is so much better than only a two week vacation to see a new area.

I'll write more about Margaret after I go to a party she is giving.

SEE YOU IN JUNE, LOVE, BOBBIE

Chapter Forty-eight

Now, That's the Life

I was flattered when Margaret Morgan seemed to take me under her wing. She was very perceptive and sensed the undercurrent of pain that still was a part of my life, although I tried to hide it.

Several times on Saturdays, Margaret invited me out to her home overlooking the shipping channel in Puget Sound between Tacoma and the rest of the world. Although I didn't give any details, I told her about my need to think things through concerning Floyd. Everything was very low key at Margaret's. Her husband was overseas someplace so just the two of us ate lunch together. Then while Margaret worked in her rose garden, I was free to relax all by myself anywhere I wished to go on the estate. I took walks in the woods, but I always ended up in the gazebo overlooking the Sound. On my second visit, Margaret joined me with her needlepoint. There we sat, enjoying the view of the water and the ships below. I was unwinding and silently praying for continued peace and contentment.

I've never had so much fun since high school. There's no one breathing down my neck trying to make sure I'm not breaking any rules. Heck, I don't even want to rebel against anything, except Floyd. Why did I ever fall for him in the first place? How am I going to avoid doing the same thing all over again? I'm doing pretty well…but there's no real temptation

205

out there in front of me. I pray that I'll be stronger than I've ever been before if I see myself getting serious with a guy. I'm going to really focus on friendship and genuine compatibility first. I'll be more concerned about a fellow's background and will compare it to mine. I know now that I can't make clear decisions when the excitement of sex is influencing my thinking.

All too soon it was time to head back to the city. Both times I thanked her for a lovely time, and drove "my" clunker down the long drive to the highway.

Several weeks later Margaret informed me that she and her husband were going to have one of their Dungeness crab dinners, and that she would be delighted if I could join them for it. She explained that it would be a party for only twelve people because that was all of the sterling silver crab tools that she had! I accepted her invitation with great anticipation.

Looks like this isn't going to be a newspaper on a picnic kind of feast! I don't know why I rated an invitation but I'm going to enjoy it to the hilt!

I arrived to discover the most elegant table in the world. A spectacular arrangement of Margaret's own roses lay low in the middle of a huge table set for twelve. The candles were thin tapers about 3 feet tall and their light reflected on the sparkling crystal wine glasses. But eclipsing all of it was the gleaming silver flatware. In addition to the usual abundant knives, forks and spoons displayed in a formal dinner, there was a whole line-up of gleaming utensils at each place to be used for securing every bit of the succulent morsels of crab, or lobster, or whatever. Each of us had our little wooden cutting block banded in silver, (to protect the china plates?), a tiny little silver hammer, silver pliers, and a variety of small forks and picks. I was absolutely spellbound.

Somehow the gracious humility of our host and hostess overcame what could have been a snobbery show of wealth. We reflected her joy at having found the lovely silver crab tools.

The dinner started out with a beautiful salad of tender young spring greens and crisp vegetables. It was dressed with a light vinaigrette. No bottles of Heinz salad dressings here! The hot buttery rolls were delicious. The second course was a creamy thick clam chowder, sprinkled with a bit of dill, appropriate for a seafood dinner. Little round oyster crackers accompanied the soup. Then we were served hot plates with some colorful steamed fresh vegetables and a savory rice pilaf on them. We passed baskets of hot crusty bread. Finally, the maids carried in huge steaming platters of chunks of Dungeness crab, in the shell, and we helped ourselves with abandon. I carefully watched Margaret and Henry to see which tools they used and when. A fresh fruit compote topped with whipped cream finished off the wonderful meal.

After a stimulating conversation in the library where dessert wines, petite fours, fine chocolates, and rich dark coffee were served, we said our reluctant farewells. I floated home, in my clunker, sure that I had experienced a slice of life that I would never see again, except in the movies.

PART SIX

Impaled,
All Over Again!

And the God of peace
will soon crush Satan
under your feet.

Romans 16:20

Chapter Forty-nine

Back Home Again In Indiana

As soon as school was out, I headed for Gary by train. It was cheaper and I wanted to be able to sneak into town without Floyd finding out I was home. I didn't ask anyone to meet the train because I wanted to walk in on the folks and take them by surprise. I had to see if they would really take me in again. I caught a cab and when we drove up into the curved driveway, I asked the cab driver to wait while I went in to the house. Sometime later as we settled down from crying and making mutual vows of eternal love, I remembered the cabby. Dad went out, got my luggage, and paid him and sent him on his way.

Mom had an uncle (in-law) named Walter Zuschke. He stood tall and stately, a stern, typical Prussian. He was a retired professor of education in Germany. He stayed with Mom and Dad while attending to business in Chicago. I had been home about two weeks. Mom and I prepared my favorite meal: a tender, savory pot roast cooked with potatoes, carrots, onions, and lots of gravy. Mom made Dad's favorite, a wilted lettuce salad with hot bacon, vinegar and sugar. Fresh green beans came out of Mom's garden...We topped it all off with our traditional celebration; chocolate cake, piled high with fluffy seven minute icing. My brother John was overseas in the Navy, but Bert, Milt and I, with Mom and Dad, were relaxing in the living room and visiting with Uncle Walter. We were all moaning about having eaten too much, which was standard for our family on a fine Sunday afternoon.

As our conversation turned to Uncle Walter's life in Germany during World War II, the door bell rang. I looked out the window, jumped up, and cried,

"Oh, no! It's Floyd!"

All conversation in the room came to a dead halt.

I drug myself to the front door and opened it.

"Hi, Bonnie, It's me again!"

"How did you find out I was home?"

"Oh, I figured it was about time for you to run back to your folks again."

"Well, I'm sorry. You're right. Here I am! So what?"

"Seriously, Bonnie, I'd like to talk with you for a little bit."

I knew that Dad had forbidden him to ever set foot in our house again, so I suggested that we sit out on the porch. Now I had sincerely promised my parents that I would never ever again have anything to do with Floyd Dubois. I know Mom and Dad were confident that I would get rid of Floyd in short order.

I have absolutely no recollection of the conversation between Floyd and me. My mind seemed to be lost in a heavy fog. I do recall feeling like I was in a strong magnetic field and was being drawn under Floyd's control again.

I had no awareness of the tension that probably permeated the living room, either then or after I walked wordlessly past everyone and back to my room. There I mechanically threw some clothes into my suitcase. I returned to where my family was waiting to see what was up, and I tonelessly announced that I was leaving with Floyd. I tried to ignore their shocked gasps and before anyone could move, I walked out to Floyd who was waiting in his car. No one had a chance to try to stop me. Apparently they knew that I was going through with it regardless of anything they could do or say.

Again Floyd took me to a hotel downtown and spent the night with me until we could find a room to rent. Mom told me later that in his professional opinion, Uncle Walter said that Floyd used "mesmerism" on me and that he had me under mind control.

Floyd and I rented a room with an old Greek widower, and I got a job teaching fourth grade in Gary. Floyd worked for his father in his construction business. Once again I had a sanctuary in my classroom while everything became intolerable at home. Once again I moved out by myself into another rented room closer to my school and once again Floyd came calling. But this time it was to tell me that he too thought that we should get a divorce. I eventually talked him into paying for it, by granting him one last favor. After he was gone I thought triumphantly,

Well, for a one-night-stand, I was a pretty expensive prostitute! Not many women can brag about that! But it was just for this one time only!

I called my lawyer, Mr. Robb, and told him I wanted to file for another divorce. And, once again, my dear parents welcomed me back home.

Chapter Fifty

In a
Dark Alley

One evening after school started, I managed to outwit Floyd,. I escaped to my lawyer's office. I flopped down in the softest chair I could see. I tried to relax. I needed to settle down. I felt safe there, for awhile, at least!

"Well, hello, Barbara!"

We had no time for formalities!

"Mr. Robb, I want to draw up a restraining order against Floyd."

"Why, Barbara? You look like you're in terrible shape! What happened?"

"I'm desperate! I'm afraid of him! You have to keep Floyd away from me!"

"Who's Floyd?"

"He's my husband! I married him after you got me that divorce from Johnny."

"I'm sorry, but there's nothing I can do about it on a Friday afternoon."

"Why not?"

"A restraining order is a legal document. It doesn't go into effect until it is registered in court. The court is closed now. I'll take care of it the first thing Monday morning."

"But, what am I going to do?

"Well, why don't you him that the restraining order is now in effect anyway. Maybe he won't know the difference."

"OK…, but I guess that means I'm on my own all weekend! Well, that's it? Thanks, anyway. Wish me luck!"

As I gathered up my stuff, Mr. Robb assured me that he would take care of it as soon as possible. Then he seemed to imply that if Floyd hurt me it would make good evidence in court! I didn't tell him that I was afraid because Floyd had a loaded gun under the front seat in his truck. I didn't want to worry him! It wasn't his problem!

"Take care, now!" he added.

I needed time to regain my composure. Reality had sobered me up. I paused at the top of the stairs as I made plans as to what to do next.

I remembered how, just an hour before, Floyd had set me up as I left school with children all around me. As soon as I came out the door, he grabbed my arm and in a soft menacing voice, he snarled,

"I'm taking you home tonight. We're leaving now, together!"

"Oh, no, we're not," I hissed! "I'm taking the bus, as usual. Mom will be waiting for me," I whispered.

He gripped my arm more tightly, and said,

"You're going with me. You don't want me to make a scene here in front of all of the kids, do you?"

I knew he meant it. I jerked my arm away from him but then went ahead and sauntered over to his truck and scrambled up into it. I didn't want to attract any attention. Once in the truck and on the way downtown I tried to think of how I could get away from him.

I remembered that the florist shop below my lawyer's office had a back door that opened directly to the stairs to the second floor. I told Floyd that I wanted to order some flowers for my mother's birthday. He parked in a lot across the alley from the office building and he deliberately escorted me to the shop with a firm grip on my elbow. He knew I would bolt if I got a chance. As he waited by the front door of the shop, I wandered around looking at the displays until I was near the back door. All of a sudden I made a dash for the stairs, ran up to the second floor and into the lawyer's office, leaving Floyd behind.

When I came out of Mr. Robb's office and started back down the stairs, I saw Floyd waiting for me. His face was bright red and twisted in anger. I marched down, trying to appear confident and in control. This time my reputation as a teacher wasn't at stake and I was determined to resist him. I coldly told him that I had signed a restraining order and that he was forbidden by law to touch me. He was smarter about such things than I thought.

"That's a lie and you know it. You're coming with me, girlie, whether you want to or not.

Floyd grabbed my arm. I winced and then whimpered in pain.

"Floyd, you're hurting me!" I cried in surprise. He had never been this mad or this violent with me before.

"That's nothing compared to what I want to do to you! You don't make a fool out of Floyd Dubois!"

I tried to twist away out of his grip but he only squeezed my arm harder. He wasn't going to let go of me this time. I was desperate because I was afraid of that loaded gun!

He started dragging me down the street to the parking lot and to his truck. I was very aware of the fact that there was a large stretch of unoccupied sand dunes between downtown Gary and the area where we lived out near Lake Michigan. I had to prevent him from taking me from the security of the city. I seriously feared for my life. I had to get away before we got to the truck, so, in the relative privacy of the deserted alley, I screamed and struggled against him. He slugged me hard in my stomach. As I bent over in pain, he grabbed my hair, jerked me upright, slapped me, and then knocked me down into a mud puddle. He was getting ready to kick me when two men stepped out of a garage to see what was going on. I signaled to them to not get involved and Floyd rushed to his truck and sped away, his tires squealing as he pulled out onto the street.

The men then came over to help me get up and to see that I was alright. I thanked them, straightened up my dirty, muddy dress and walked to the bus stop at Fifth Avenue and Broadway. I stood in a shadow there so as not to attract attention. As soon as the bus doors opened, I made a dash up into the bus and grabbed a seat right behind the driver for a safe ride home. And that was the last I ever talked to Floyd Dubois.

Neither of us had to appear in court when the divorce was granted, but for some time Floyd continued to go to the Unitarian Church where we had been going together ever since we first met. He sat in the back, behind me. I felt like his eyes were boring into the back of my head but I never acknowledged his presence. Finally even that "harassment" stopped.

At last I was off of the horns of the devil...,or was he only the devil's impersonator?

Part Seven

Impaled...
In Conclusion

"If you are going to be used by God,
He will take you through
a multitude of experiences
that are not meant for you at all, they
are meant to make you useful in His
hands, and to enable you to understand
what transpires in
other souls so that you will never be
surprised at what you come across."

From "My Utmost for His Highness"
by Oswald Chambers. C1935, p.230
Dodd Mead & Company and Barbour and Company, Inc.
164 Mill Street, Box 1219,Westwood, NJ., 07675.

Chapter Fifty-one

But Why, Lord?

What in my social development contributed to my defiance in dating and marrying Johnny? Why was I so vulnerable to Floyd's flattery? Where did my hearing loss figure in? Where did my life-saving stability through teaching come from?

Insecurity with Boys

As I looked back at the writing I've done, I began to knit together those parts in my past that seemed to contribute to the development of my self-image. This self-identity issue had a great influence on decisions I made and how I lived my life.

When I was removed enough from the conflict to try to figure out the causes for such a dramatic rebellion as described in this book, I remembered my very real insecurity with some of the boys in high school. I got along very well and was comfortable with the boys that I thought looked on me as a good friend. I found myself in a counseling position between couples or the lovelorn. Boys confided in me about the girls that they wanted to date and wanted encouragement to set up a date. I enjoyed, and had no trouble hearing, whispered conversations, especially during study hall, with some of the boys about life and philosophy and religion. I helped, and received help, on homework and I even taught several of the guys to dance on our sun porch at home. It was all purely platonic. Until Johnny came along no one asked me for a date. Before that I would never admit being interested in any certain boy. I feared rejection so much I couldn't ask anyone to set me up with a guy. I thought flirting was naughty. I didn't have a slim, trim figure like the popular girls had and I had absolutely no confidence in my ability to attract a boyfriend.

My Appearance

My dimples and/or reddish blond hair frequently attracted complements from strangers. I was insulated from teasing by peers about my red hair, by reminding myself that they were just jealous. One day Grandma caught me as a 6 or 7 year old, standing on her bed, stark naked, and looking at myself in her dresser mirror. I was totally ignoring the fact that I didn't have any clothes on. I wasn't ashamed of my nakedness before her. I was trying to see if my dimples were like Shirley Temple's. She was a very popular child movie star of about my age. I was checking out my dimples, turning this way and that and trying on different smiles to see them best. All my dear grandma said to me was, "Don't worry. They'll just turn to wrinkles some day." She and my mother were carefully combating any tendency I might have to be vain.

Our conversations about my appearance with my parents went something like this: "You look very nice in that new dress" or "I was so proud of you last night." No one ever told me or my sister or brothers that we were pretty or handsome. All of the adults in my family wanted to make sure that we didn't act like we were "stuck-up." It was fine to be proud of accomplishments but not of our bodies or of physical beauty.

For most of my life, I honestly didn't know that I was pretty or physically special in any way.

PUBERTY

The shape of our bodies and evidence of puberty brought shame and embarrassment instead of pride and self-confidence.

"In my day as a flapper," Mom told me, "we didn't want anyone to see our bust line. It was the fashion to have flat chests just like a boy, so we wrapped a cloth tightly around our chests to flatten down our breasts as much as possible."

Perhaps some of that attitude still existed in her as she made my dresses all through school. In the fittings she always tried to camouflage my breasts or allow the tops to be "nice and roomy" so that my bust line didn't show. I spent most of my life, even into adulthood, with my shoulders hunched forward to minimize my breasts even though they weren't unusually large.

I always had a "weight problem". In high school Mom and I frequently went on diets together as she encouraged me to lose some weight. I was probably never more than 20 pounds overweight, but those pounds loomed large in the self image of a teen-ager.

I was ashamed of my body until at least age 70! By then I accepted it as natural for my age, at last!

SEXUALITY

Over the dinner table one night Dad released his frustration and disgust when he said about his co-workers on the fire department, "Those men down at the station are so disgusting. They sit out there in front of the open doors of the station and they undress every woman that goes by. Some of the sluts strut by frequently. The men make crude jokes among themselves. I can't stand it so I go inside, pick up my book, and read."

Forever after, whenever I went to the fire station to see my dad, I always approached the station from the side on the way to the back door. Then I didn't have to walk by the men who were sitting outside with the front legs of their chairs propped up in the air, watching all of the women who went by. For the rest of my life I always found it very difficult to walk in front of a group of men. Sometimes I wish I had been taught to "strut my stuff", too, and not worry about acting "suggestive".

Commenting on feminine wiles, Mom said,

"Did you notice how she rolls her eyes as she talks? Wasn't it disgusting? So dramatic and so brazen. I have to scold Bertha (my younger sister) for it all the time. I just don't know where she gets that."

One time when I was in high school, a new girl moved into our area and instantly became very popular. She had a joyous, bubbly personality and I told Mom I wished I could be like that with the boys.

"Gilbert, this new girl that Bobbie envies so…I think we knew her mother when we were young adults.

"Yes, I know who you mean. She sure was popular with the men."

"She was always laughing and flirting and had "round heels".

Mom scornfully said it looked like her daughter had "It" just like her mother did. I figured out what they meant by "round heels" but when I asked what "It" was, they either couldn't or wouldn't tell me. Since their tone of voice implied disapproval, I decided it was a sexy or inviting attitude that proper girls didn't engage in. It seemed to me that any show of femininity was to be scorned. Only sensible and dignified, or gender- neutral behavior was acceptable in my parent's eyes and they were so proud of me. I was always such a Good Girl (perfect) until I started dating Johnny.

After I started dating, Mom was always fearful for me and frequently reminded me that boys and men couldn't be trusted. She said over and over, "If you give a boy an inch, he'll take a mile". She never warned me that eventually, after some heavy petting with Johnny, I might want to give him that mile! I learned from her and Dad that any behavior designed to attract the opposite sex was "Asking for it", so I never smiled at or acted friendly to any of those big guys, the athletes, in school because I was afraid of them. I guess I wasn't afraid of the studious boys and the more cerebral ones because I thought they had more on their minds than just sex.

Little did I know that my comfort level with boys such as it was, was going to take a nosedive as we got older.

Chapter Fifty-two

My
Hearing Loss

Despite several factors that possibly contributed to my lack of social confidence in my early years, I recognized recently what a serious social handicap my hearing loss was for me for much of my life. It actually was the greatest factor, and I can't blame anyone for it, including myself!

I was fortunate in that I grew up never considering myself as handicapped. I thought of physical handicaps and mental handicaps as things that could be seen and therefore caused others to treat the handicapped in a condescending manner. Since my "problem" wasn't visible, I didn't expect or experience anyone treating me any differently than they treated other "normal" children.

When I was a pre-schooler Mom and Aunt Mary continually scolded me for saying "Huh?" all of the time. They thought it was just a bad habit that I had developed.

In first grade I found out that in order to hear the teacher, I always had to ask for a front seat. I took special classes in lip-reading when I was in Junior High, but because I wasn't totally dependent on it, I never became truly proficient. The skill became more of a prop than anything else.

Since my loss was greatest in the lower registers, as the boys' voices in high school began to change and get deeper, I became more and more uncomfortable trying to hear what they were saying to me. I strained and I tried to use my lip reading but I had to work at it and I couldn't just sit back and enjoy the conversation. I couldn't take part in the repartee. I was afraid I wouldn't pick up the innuendos, the jokes, the comments made under the breath. I was afraid that I would or wouldn't laugh at the right time or that I would use an inappropriate facial expression when I shouldn't. I tried to imitate what was showing on other people's faces so that I would be projecting the right emotions. Most of the time it was just too much trouble. I avoided quiet one-on-one conversations and one-liners with boys completely, unless I already knew that they were friends and that I would be able to hear their voices.

Then I went away to college and all the voices of the fellows were mature. My hearing became more of a problem, socially. In an effort to read lips I focused on men's faces so intently that it was impossible to relax and enjoy myself, and them. It was easiest to stay in the sorority house on date nights and write letters or play cards with the other losers than it was to try to "catch" a guy. I didn't even accept any blind dates because I couldn't trust my hearing.

Even in my childhood, hearing aids were available for those who were in desperate need. The ones that my mother, my grandmother, and my great aunt wore were powered by two big C cell batteries, about 1 ¼ inch in diameter and 2 ¼ inch long and very heavy. Mom carried the batteries in a cloth bag that she pinned to the lower side edge of her girdle. A wire from the batteries ran under her dress and was connected to a microphone that was about the size of a pack of cigarettes or a deck of cards. The microphone had a clip on it so she could clip it to her bra. Then she stuffed it, her "squeal box" (feedback noise) out of sight between her mature and ample breasts. From there, two wires came around under her dress to pass under one of her armpits to the nape of her neck. At that point the wires separated and were attached to an ear mold in each ear. It's no wonder hearing aids weren't proposed for me when I was a child! And they would have sounded like a death knell to a teen-ager. That's when someone might have been considered "handicapped." Even today, 2011, a more modern form of the bulky hearing aids is used by anyone designated as profoundly deaf.

My hearing deteriorated as I approached age thirty and I was fitted successfully with a hearing aid. By then an aid was self-contained, battery and microphone built into the ear mold or hung inconspicuously behind the ear. They had become possible through the miniaturization created as a spin-off of the space program and our efforts to put a man on the moon. I didn't try to hide my aid. I openly admitted that I needed all the help I could get.

After we moved to California in 1966, my audiologist convinced me that it was now time to wear an aid in each ear. I had accepted the first aid with grace and thankfulness. I didn't know any trauma at that necessity because I still had one good ear to fall back on. But when I was told that the "good" ear needed help too, I cried all of the way home. Then I experienced all of the emotional pain that cause others to avoid wearing hearing aids. Finally I became grateful for mine, both of them, because I knew that if it weren't for that help, long before it would be time to retire, I would be sitting home, reading and knitting beside the fireplace.

Chapter Fifty-three

Teaching

As for teaching with a hearing loss like mine, I managed very well. My elementary school students had higher pitched voices than men. I maintained a very quiet room whenever I was working with my small instruction groups and in that way I could hear them, and my students developed good study habits at their desks. I enjoyed activity periods with them and their chatter didn't bother me, maybe because the volume didn't fully register with me! Grades four, five, and six, which I enjoyed most, had strong clear voices. They used longer sentences than primary students did. I could use context when trying to hear them. And maybe most important, I wasn't shy about telling students that I couldn't hear them because I taught them it was their duty to speak up clearly when we had class discussions. My students probably had the best diction in the whole school!

My foremost identity, absolutely constant throughout my life, was that of a teacher. Mom and Dad ingrained that role in me from childhood and will be "me" as long as I live. As a teacher, at last, I was supremely self-confident and very much in control. Today, even my writing is motivated by the teacher in me.

Early in the second semester of my senior year in high school our principal, Mr. Reid called me into his office. I stood before him in fear and trembling. Not really! We were good friends.

"Barbara, it looks like you have some free time every afternoon?"

"Yes, sir, I've been going home at 1:00. I've fulfilled all of the requirements for graduation because I doubled up all the way through high school."

"Well, I have a suggestion for you that we thought you might enjoy." He came around his desk and perched on the corner of it so he wouldn't seem so tall and formidable. I remained standing, curious as to what was up. He continued,

"Mrs. Frederickson, the district psychologist is doing some work with some fourth grade boys. They haven't made good progress because of various behavior problems. They come from troubled homes, things like that. She needs a student helper in the afternoons. Do you think you would like to help her for an hour each day?"

"That sounds interesting."

"There's more to it than just that. Mrs. Frederickson can only be out here on Monday, Wednesday, and Friday. You will work with her on those days and you'll work alone with the boys on Tuesdays and Thursdays."

"Oh, wow! Do think I'll be able to handle them all by myself?"

"We have no doubt about it. It will be only a small group, just 5 or 6 boys. They are really nice boys and want to please."

"How will I know what to do with them on my own? Just observe what Mrs. Frederickson does and try to do as she does?"

"Yes, and she will leave lesson plans for you to follow, just like teachers leave for their substitutes."

"Well…O K, I'll give it a try…It's going to be a new kind of challenge, isn't it?'

"Yes, and we wouldn't have suggested it if we didn't feel you could handle it. You can report to Mrs. Frederickson in room 10 at 1:00, beginning Monday afternoon."

He stood up. We shook hands as he dismissed me. I tried to walk out sedately and not let him know I was so excited I wanted to take the stairs two at a time on the way down to the front door. I practically ran all the way home. I burst through the kitchen door shouting,

"Mama! Mama! Guess what Mr. Reid wants me to do!"

From that day on, I was on my way to becoming a teacher. My dreams of becoming a linguist just flew out the window. I had thought that way I could get a job in a foreign embassy and do a lot of traveling all over the world. But now, I said I wasn't so sure I had a lot of talent in learning languages anyway.

After I graduated from Indiana University and got my first class, I knew I was where I belonged. Teaching became my reason for existence, my service to humanity, and my lifeblood. Later, as I went through great mental turmoil, paramount in my thinking was that whatever was going on in my personal life, I must protect my ability to support myself through teaching.

But it was much more than that. I deeply loved each one of my students. I knew my students perhaps even better than their aunts and uncles. I thrived on the love and respect that they returned to me. I was sincerely dedicated to helping them do the very best that they were capable of. I worked hard at my teaching, carrying home papers to grade almost every night. At times I even let my homework intrude too much into my home life and my attention to a spouse. In times of great personal stress I was able to go into the classroom and completely ignore what might be going on at home and focus exclusively on my responsibilities to my students. This probably helped protect me from even greater mental agony.

I have always enjoyed teaching. I consider it a God-given talent and am very thankful to Him for it.

Put on the full armor of God that
you may be able to stand firm
against the schemes of the devil."
*"Stand firm therefore, having girded your
loins with truth, and having put on the
breastplate of righteousness, and having
shod your feet with the preparation
of the gospel of peace; in addition to all,
taking up the shield of faith
with which you will be able to extinguish
all the flaming arrows of the evil one.
And take the helmet of salvation
and the sword of the Spirit, which
is the word of God,"...

Ephesians 6:11, 13-17

Chapter Fifty-four

The
Battleground

As I was growing up, I thought my Christian role was to be good and kind and loving to others. I thought that would earn praise and love from everyone around me. I knew about heaven, and if there was one, my good deeds would insure my entry there some day. I relied on my memory of the childhood teachings of my Sunday school teachers. I'm sure it was nebulous. I knew only that God loved me and that He would protect me from evil.

From the time I started dating I was at odds with my parents on that subject. In high school I went against their advice by going steady with my first boyfriend for two and a half years. We became engaged before going off to college. After giving him back his ring during my freshman year, I dated a non-Christian and considered marrying him. Mom and Dad were so concerned that they made a special trip to campus to meet him. When they arrived back home, Dad asked a favorite high school teacher to write to me and advise me to stop dating him. I accepted her advice and broke up with him, I dated several other college students for awhile but Mom and Dad objected to every student I brought home for them to meet. I think they thought I was rebelling against their Christian values and our cultural morality. I didn't limit my dating to men with strong

Christian commitment because I didn't have one myself. I felt very guilty about my inability to practice sexual abstinence.

Many years later I recognized that these changes in my behavior and personality were the result of me not really being worried about "sin" or disobedience, not only of my parents, but of God, Himself. My definition of sin was limited to gross things like murder.

As I became involved with Floyd Dubois, a much greater spiritual and moral battle began to take place in my mind. On one hand I was deeply committed to my understanding of God's love and His protection of me. I knew His requirement of obedience to His commands in the Bible, and I knew that my attitudes and actions were becoming more and more ungodly. I knew I didn't deserve His love, but I just wasn't able or willing to let God's standards rule over me.

It was strange how Floyd commanded my absolute attention whenever he talked to me. He always used a very soft voice even when I asked him, over and over again, to speak up to me. He kept me off balance and anxious. That was just part of his controlling me, psychologically. I allowed Floyd to break down all of my defenses. At times he seemed to have an almost hypnotic control over me. I became compliant to his will and influence, even when I knew they ran counter to the family values that my parents had instilled in me.

For almost two years I struggled in this war between good and evil. Later I recognized it as a serious battle between God and Satan for the possession of my mind and soul. During much of my late teens and early adulthood I expressed an ungodly spirit of rebellion. It encompassed much more than the usual teenager's need to exist independently outside the protection of home and family circle, to not draw his or her identity from parents, or to stand as a growing independent adult.

I confessed, and cried, and pleaded with God to forgive me for the lack of sexual abstinence with Johnny. Later on, time and time again,

I promised Him that I would break the hold that Floyd seemed to have to control me and his ability to bend me to his will.

Finally, I realized that I was 22 years old and still engaged in a self-destructive moral rebellion that was very painful to my loved ones and to me. It threatened my reputation and security as a teacher. It brought me into conflict with all I had been taught about admirable behavior. I just wasn't willing to conform to what I knew was right.

It was phenomenal that between these periods of mental turmoil, I enjoyed periods of the most astounding peace and contentment. These were completely unrelated to my secret agonies in every way. It was almost like I was leading two very separate lives. During the day I was able to focus completely on my students in my classroom. At other times, when alone, I thoroughly enjoyed Seattle and the Pacific Northwest. I believe that these hours were God-given times that enabled me to maintain my sanity throughout all of the pain of the opposition of my parents and two failed marriages.

When I fought back and attempted to break the stranglehold that kept me in bondage and misery, I remembered my early training and God's commands in both the Old and New Testaments of the Bible.

In the absence of spiritual guidance, which I would not accept at the time, psychological counseling gave me the insight and strength to break free from the satanic power that enslaved me. I was released from that influence to preserve me until a later time when I would be willing to humbly accept His Son, Jesus Christ, as my Lord and Savior.

What does the Lord your God
require of you, but to fear the Lord
your God,
to walk in all His ways
and to serve the Lord your God
with all your heart and with all your soul,
and to keep the Commandments of the Lord
and His statutes
which I command you today
for your own good?

Deuteronomy 10:12-15

Chapter Fifty-five

I
Believe...

My sister knows me better than any other human being. After reading the last few chapters of my manuscript, she wrote,

"Your honesty and openness has amazed me. In order to share your love of Christ, you have been willing to peel back so many layers of what has made you, YOU.

I replied, *"Thanks. You know what courage I had to summon in the beginning. My focus has been on honesty all the way through this story... even when it hurt... even when it was embarrassing! Now, it won't be fully me unless I share some of the cause and effect ideas that have occurred to me. I never would have exposed myself like I that if my intent was to just entertain. The loss of my privacy would have been too big a price to pay."*

My recent observations, my growing maturity and a deep, constant faith in Jesus Christ and the power of the Holy Spirit, leads me to present what I could call, "The moral to the story is..."

As I review how God <u>did</u> work in my life, I came up with an impressive list:

I believe that despite other negative factors, it was my hearing loss that was <u>the</u> major factor in preventing me from developing a healthy sense of self worth. That was something no one could have any control over.

I believe that my mom and dad deeply loved each one of us and did their very best to give us Christian principles and guidance to live by.

I believe that when we left the church of my childhood, Mom and Dad did not replace it with a church that had a strong doctrinal message. They did not require me to attend Sunday school or youth group activities where their teachings would have been reinforced.

I believe that long before children become adolescents, it is important to instill concepts about Christian dating that will hopefully guide them as they become teen-agers. Among them is the biblical command to not marry an unbeliever (unequally yoked).

I believe that parents and spiritual leaders should help a teen develop a list of desirable qualities to be found in a spouse, to be used seriously by a young person as a screening device in <u>all</u> dating. There should be no such thing as "casual" dating. One never knows when the love bug will bite, and when it happens, sometimes reason and common sense fly out the window!

I believe that teen romances should be respected as training grounds for monogamy and possible marriage, and can lead to the marriage of lifetime partners that the Lord has ordained.

I believe parents must pray and <u>trust</u> God to provide His choice of a mate to their child in His good timing.

I believe if parents trust God and His sovereignty they would have confidence that a young couple can grow together under the guidance of the Holy Spirit and that cultural and social differences are not disasters written in stone.

I believe intense negative parental pressure has the potential of driving a teen in the wrong direction and may even contribute to later marital problems.

I believe that church youth groups can be important training grounds for serious dating. There teens have the opportunity to develop close relationships with others of similar backgrounds. In healthy church group activities, teens naturally pair up but the emphasis should be on fluidity of friendships and group events rather than on formal dating. The informality of dating in church youth groups allows the exploration of friendships with each other without the commitment of going steady. There the development of a healthy sense of self worth and the social confidence helps offset youthful insecurities with the opposite sex. Church groups frequently contribute to the nucleus of social groups in high schools enabling members to become part of the "in" group even outside of church.

I believe that if solo (unsupervised) dating can be delayed, couples would not have the privacy that Johnny and I had…the privacy that leads to intense necking and sexual exploring. I also believe that boys, as well as girls, be taught to consider it their responsibility to maintain control over the intensity of their love-making.

Of course I am not so naïve as to believe that had I been active in a church group as a teen, I would have been able to successfully practice sexual abstinence. But I believe that going steady at an early age, with the intimate privacy that is available in today's dating scene, fosters premature sexual experimentation and puts enormous pressure on young people to become sexually involved.

I believe that genuine unity under Christ as the head of the household gives a married couple a stability that cannot be experienced any other way. Children must be taught to not even date others who would not treasure this unity. What grief it would have saved me if I had been obedient to this commandment from the very beginning!

I believe that, strange as this may sound, given the hellish three years of my early adult life, from childhood I always knew that God loved me and I thought that He would protect me.

I believe there is a difference between God protecting me and God preserving me. God didn't <u>protect</u> me from those disastrous years with Floyd. God <u>preserved</u> me despite the fact that I was thumbing my nose at Him in everything that had to do with my personal life. Perhaps He was also preserving me when I seriously considered throwing myself in front of a passing car, but didn't go through with it!

I believe that even though most of my prayers were penitent pleadings to reverse the consequences of bad moral choices that I made, I still remained confident of God's love and His ability to answer prayers. I heard recently that many times we sow wild oats during the week and go to church on Sunday to pray for a crop failure! I guess that was me, when I prayed, or when I went to church!

I believe that teaching was my God-given talent and was what gave meaning to my life and held me together emotionally. My classroom was my physical and emotional island of security, confidence, and love. Despite all that was going on at wherever I was currently calling "home", I really was able to separate the trauma and pain in my personal life from my responsibilities to my students. I was proud of the dedication that I enjoyed in teaching. I was an excellent teacher, and I knew it.

I believe the islands of peace in my classroom and in Seattle were God-given times that enabled me to hang onto my sanity and avoid an emotional breakdown.

I believe that, despite times of deep agony, I thoroughly enjoyed

Seattle, the weather, and the North West. My memories of Seattle are dominated by beauty, and it is as if Floyd and his influence took place on another planet.

I believe God caused me to enter secular psychological counseling for myself twice as a part of His plan for preserving me until the day that I could be useful to Him. Each time I was consciously confused and could admit it, I turned to the only source of help that I would accept at that time. Each time my counselor was able to help me see the truly disastrous road that I was traveling with Floyd and to give me respite.

As for Floyd Dubois, I believe that if I had been wearing the 'full armor of God', I would have immediately recognized any inappropriate behavior on his part and would have done whatever was necessary to avoid him completely.

I believe that Floyd Dubois embodied a sinister and evil force that I succumbed to. I didn't know about the reality of Satan's opposition to all things holy and godly. I allowed Floyd to enter my world through sexual innuendos and the consequence was 2 ½ years of real emotional turmoil and pain as long as I was under his control.

I believe that abortion, or the killing of a child, for the mother's convenience, is a personal and national sin and a scourge today. If babies were not aborted, women would not be carrying the life-long emotional scars caused by the inhuman killing of their own offspring.

I believe that today children are having children, long before they are mature enough to care for them and provide for them. The divorce rate has increased, the marriage rate is decreasing because of defiance of the sanctity of marriage. Innocent children are suffering in the destruction of the family. Families of irresponsible fathers and single parent families are at a serious financial disadvantage, contributing to the ratio of poverty in the country.

I believe that many young people today proceed on a self-indulgent way with no guilty conscience as to pre-marital sex and that this route has led to sexual promiscuity, an increase in sexual diseases, and children born out of wedlock. It has fostered irresponsible fatherhood, leaving children to never know the security of an intact home life with both loving parents.

I believe the defiance or ignorance of biblical commandments in regards to sexual behavior is contributing to disastrous national and societal dysfunction, and that is causing our family values to fall by the wayside. I guess, in addition to being very penitent for my ignorance and rebellion, I am seriously worried about where this same defiance is leading our country.

I believe that in addition to my teaching, God had a purpose for my life. I became useful to Him by accumulating all that I had experienced, both good and bad, distilling it and using it in teaching, in loving my family and friends, and in a God-honoring counseling program at church. Because of my experiences and my faith I have become helpful to others who seek help in dealing with current disasters in their lives and in living God-centered lives.

Originally, I didn't know how to gain the assurance of God's blessings. Later I learned that:

A. I must accept His Son, Jesus Christ as my Lord and Master.
B. I could turn to Him and the Holy Spirit for guidance.
C. If I did accept Christ, I would find it much easier to obey God's rules for godly living because the Power of the Holy Spirit would be behind me and living within me.
D. I would really enjoy keeping in touch with God through prayer and daily Bible study (I like to call this "Bible Application").

E. In order to do God's will, I have to run all of my motives and actions through the filter of doing everything for His glory alone.

AND, despite all of the pain and agony and defiance that my parents endured, they continued to love me, to support me emotionally, and to take me back, over and over again. I knew I could <u>always</u> come back home whenever I was willing to humble myself and move forward in repentance and love. For that I will treasure their love and respect forever. I am very, very grateful that they, just like God, never gave up on me.

To Him
Be dominion
forever
and
ever.

Amen 1 Peter 5: 11, NAS

Epilogue
The Holy Spirit

After my husband, Carl Boatright, and I moved from Indiana to California, I accepted Jesus Christ as my Lord and Savior and became a "born-again Christian". The Holy Spirit led me into a teaching mission and service to the Lord at church. I continued to teach in the public schools but I knew in my heart, that as a silent witness, I was bringing glory to God even there. After an early retirement from the elementary classroom, I was able to lead and teach women's groups at church and in my senior community.

After extensive training at church I was granted my church's certificate as a lay counselor. As such, I enjoyed my voluntary service to some of those who in desperation turned to the church for help in working through serious personal and marital problems. I knew that God allowed me to foul up and suffer through years of defiance and personal agony as preparation for fulfilling His purpose in me and, by extension, in others. All the while I knew that it was the Holy Spirit, alone, that gave me the power and guidance to serve God in this manner.

There is much in between "Impaled" and the end of my life story. But another summation of who I am and who I have been took place in 2006. My husband and I celebrated our Fiftieth Wedding Anniversary with our families and friends! I was proud that through spiritual strength and greater maturity, I had learned to maintain a mutually loving relationship with my husband. At our reception I surprised myself with a willingness to disclose a well kept secret. Our guests were shocked when I revealed that this was the third marriage for each of us! Because of this, I declared that God had given us more reason to celebrate than most couples who reach that milestone. We declared our undying love for each other and everyone is living happily ever after!

My Prayer: May God say of me:
For the report of your obedience
Has reached to all;
therefore I am rejoicing over you,
but I want you to be wise
in what is good,
and innocent in what is evil.

Romans 16:19